MEND YOUR ENGLISH

MEND YOUR ENGLISH

or

What You Should Have Been
Taught At Primary School

•

Ian Bruton-Simmonds

International
Edition

PUBLICATIONS

London – Edinburgh

To the following, the author and publisher gratefully acknowledge permission to quote:

The Harrap Publishing Group for quotation from MY PHILOSOPHY OF INDUSTRY by Henry Ford,

Harry N. Abrams, Inc. for quotation from ABRAHAM LINCOLN: HIS SPEECHES AND WRITINGS by Roy P. Basler,

Lawrence & Wishart Ltd., for quotations from ANTONIO GRAMSCI: SELECTIONS FROM THE PRISON NOTEBOOKS, Edited and translated by Quintin Hoare and Geoffrey Nowel Smith,

Oxford University Press for quotation from MODERN ENGLISH USAGE by H.W. Fowler,

St. Martin's Press Incorporated for quotation from FORTRESS WITHOUT A ROOF: THE ALLIED BOMBING OF THE THIRD REICH by Wilbur H. Morrison,

and the author gratefully records his obligation to Mademoiselle Christine Penet for her compilation of Index and Glossary.

IVY PUBLISHING
72 Hyperion House, Somers Road, London, SW2 1HZ
9a Warrender Park Crescent, Edinburgh EH91DX
and at Sydney and Johannesburg

First published 1990
Second printing 1991/1
Third printing 1991/2
Fourth printing 1993/3
Fifth printing 1994/11
Sixth printing 1997/6
Seventh printing 1999/10

Typeset by Gutenberg Book Printers

ISBN 0-620-15019-X

Contents

Illustrations

Preface

This booklet contains the substance of the weekly series IMPROVE YOUR ENGLISH that ran in the Johannesburg SOWETAN from April 1983 to March 1984.

In writing that series I had in mind two classes of reader: those who have English as a second language, and those to whom English is mother-tongue – and both classes, through realization of the inadequacy of their schooling, desire improvement. Hence this booklet is not for absolute beginners.

For the first class of reader there is a comprehensive glossary, which follows each article page by page (as on this page), explaining at the bottom of a page every word that is likely to puzzle a tiro. Another device to speed learning is a quick page-to-page cross reference. For example, in the margin of page 9 is the number 15. This means that on page 15 the subject being presented on page 9 is also presented, and in the margin of page 15 is the number 9 in line with that subject. All subjects are under one of four headings: General, Style, Vocabulary, or Grammar.

There are a few key examples of good and bad opposed to each other. With these the good example precedes the bad, on

---

comprehensive = that contains much: large
desire = to have a strong wish for: to long for
device = plan: invention
glossary = explanations
grammar = rules for the best use of a language
inadequacy = not enough: what is not sufficient
key = powerful in opening up. (In this case opening up our understanding)
series = the joining of things in a certain order

35 100, 150, 200, 250, 300 is a series
    250, 150, 300, 200, 100 is not
    Much thought went into the *order* of the original SOWETAN articles, and that order has been kept for this booklet
style = special manner of writing or speaking that shows its character or quality. "Proper words in proper places make the true definition of a style", said a great English writer. Good style comes of good taste
substance = the most important subject-matter
tiro = not an absolute beginner, but one who has still to learn a lot. From Latin *tiro* ... a young soldier: a recruit
vocabulary = the words one has. A person with few words has a poor vocabulary. A person with many words that he uses not to their meaning has a faulty vocabulary

1

the principle that the good, seen first, arouses commonsense to see the bad sooner.

For those who want to climb higher than the primary-level of this booklet there are recommendations for further reading — and a few disapprovals of certain modern books that I think needlessly complicated or misleading. But I trust that no good scholar will accept my adverse opinions until he has checked those books himself!

Sufficient grammar is relatively easy to acquire. Any normal primary-school child can be taught it. This booklet, using the minimum of terminology, makes that acquisition easy. Correct grammar, however, is only a step to more important things. Good taste is the prized goal, and good taste comes only through good reading and intelligent listening. If this little guide points you to good books, and alerts you to bad reading, bad broadcasting, bad advertising and bad teaching, it will fulfil my second-highest hope. My highest hope is that the problem presented in Appendix II will soon be triumphantly solved.

---

acquire = to gain by one's own seeking ⎫ Both from Latin
acquisition = what is got by one's own effort ⎭ *acquirere* ... to seek for
adverse = against: opposite in position. From Latin *adversus* ... standing opposite like an enemy
precedes = goes before. From Latin *praecedere* ... to go before
relatively = compared with something else. (In this context, with Style & Vocabulary)
sufficient = enough
taste = judgement of quality. One with poor taste for food is likely to eat rubbish and not know that it is rubbish. Here it means the sense to know what is beautiful or ugly
terminology = words special to a subject

2

Introduction

"English is the first necessity for a scientist," said the Director of the Soviet Space Research, Roald Sagdeyev.

Indeed, today English is man's most powerful tool of thinking. It is this not only because it is the world's most widespread language, but because *great* thinkers over hundreds of years have built its literature with their most polished thoughts, and so made for the ordinary man who has good English, a razor-sharp instrument for communication.

Those who blunt this instrument (particularly through broadcasting) spoil a treasure that belongs to us and our children, and they should be classed with the most dangerous public enemies, and condemned to ridicule.

Each bad example in this booklet represents a large family of errors or inferiorities. Each is so gross that, once seen, it stands naked and ridiculous, and its many silly relatives are more easily recognised.

STYLE

Prominent Politician: It is my honest and sincere belief . . .

☐ It goes without saying that a belief is sincere, even if it is idiotic; and a man who tells you he is honest cheapens both his honesty and his intelligence. The ridiculousness of the utterance is clear if one changes it to:

☐ It is my insincere and dishonest belief . . .

discerning = able to recognize the difference between excellent, good, mediocre and bad. From Latin *discernere* . . . to separate
gross = clearly stupid. From Latin *grossus* . . . thick
literature = what is still read with pleasure by a discerning public after the writer is dead.
represents = stands for
ridicule = mocking laughter From Latin *ridere* . . . to laugh
ridiculous = deserving ridicule
sincere = not pretended: pure

VOCABULARY

President Canaan Banana of Zimbabwe called insurgents *"criminal* gangsters". One does not tell more about a criminal by saying that he is a *criminal* criminal". (See *gangster* in Glossary)

GRAMMAR

Well-known broadcaster: ... love from George, Lois and *I*.
Wrong. *I* should be *me*. If he had left out George and Lois and said ... "... love from *I*", the error would have hit him.

In the same family is the mistake, rife among school-children: *Me* and George went to the shops. Correct grammar changes "Me" to "I"; and good manners and correct idiom put *George* before *I*:

George and I went to the shops.

(105) As you see from the margin, this matter is dealt with on page 105

STYLE

First prize for commercial inanity goes to the patter telephonic greeting "Thank you for calling" that was spawned by American retailing and is now spread over the English-speaking world. The greeting is a mix of untruth and inefficiency.

A business telephone should be answered immediately with the name of the firm. Thanks should come only after it is known for what the caller is to be thanked. Surely, the thank-worthiness of the following caller is nil:

"Thank you for calling. Gush, Grovel & Smirk."

"This is a holdup. My mate's got a gun pointed at your hea Cut your 'phone off now, or he'll blow your brains out."

---

gangster = a member of a gang of violent criminals
idiom = the peculiar (special) character of. From Greek *idios* ... own; personal.
inane = without sense; meaningless; foolish. From Latin *inanis* ... empty
patter = speech repeated hurriedly and mechanically with no thought whatever
rife = in plenty

I

The scope of language

"Believe it, my good friend, to love truth for truth's sake is the principal part of human perfection in this world and the seed-plot of all other virtues," said the philosopher John Locke.

There can be no love of truth without scrupulous respect for accuracy.

The chief end of language is *accurate* transfer of thought from one mind to another, and its greatest potency is its ability through some of its words and phrases to make a man's thoughts more accurate; and the greater the man's intelligence, the greater the power of language to help him. "Speak, that I may *see* thee... No glass renders a man's form or likeness so true as his speech," says Ben Jonson. "A man's character appears more by his words than, as some think it does, by his looks," says Plutarch.

If, as has been said, the human brain is the most complicated thing in the universe, then language, as the principal expression of its intelligence, is the most wonderful thing in the universe.

Ben Jonson (born 1572 died 1637) English playwright and poet
"Whose true scope, if you would know it,
In all his poems still hath been this measure,
To mix profit with your pleasure."

From the prologue of his play VOLPONE.

He was a good friend of Shakespeare, who acted in at least one of his plays. He is regarded by some as the greatest writer of English comedy, Shakespeare not excepted
Plutarch (born about 46 died about 125) Greek historian. His LIVES OF THE NOBLE GRECIANS AND ROMANS is one of the most influential works of Western Civilization John Dryden's translation has made it an English classic
potency = strength: power
scope = widest intention: main aim before the mind
scrupulous = takes trouble even over small matters
seedplot = special place for seeds to grow
universe = the whole of creation from the furthest star and beyond to you

VOCABULARY

Claim — to demand as <u>one's due</u>: to assert and demand recognition of (an alleged) right: the <u>demand</u> of a <u>due</u>.

This is the only word in English that carries the force of what is underlined. Alas, its general misuse by journalists, politicians, commentators and others has almost killed its special use.

claimed responsibility for... rather... took responsibility for
claimed he was ill... rather... said he was ill, or maintained he was ill, or contended he was ill.

Other words to consider before using "claim" are *assert* (*assertions* rather than "claims"), *aver, contend, insist, demand, affirm, hold.*

Fact = A thing known to be true. Hence *all* facts are true. The report below would have been better with *relevant* fact, or *unbiased* fact, or better still, to have nothing with "fact".

From a news bulletin of the SABC:

"The SA Ambassador to the United States, Dr Brand Fourie, has sent a telegram to NEWSWEEK in New York objecting to a front-page article in the magazine's latest issue. The report deals with alleged suppression of Blacks in South Africa, and various unsubstantiated *claims* [allegations] are made. Dr Fourie says in the telegram that the allegations create a distorted image of SA society, and are a blatant misrepresentation of the Government's domestic policy. Dr Fourie says the article is little more than a jumbled assortment of inaccuracies which fail to recognise the SA Government's attempts at solving problems peacefully. He says NEWSWEEK has an obligation *towards* readers throughout the world to publish the *true* facts, and consequently he will submit a detailed written account of the *true* facts to the magazine's editor."

allegation = what was asserted but not proved
alleged = asserted but not proved
SA = South African
SABC = South African Broadcasting Corporation

"... obligation *towards*" is wrong idiom. Correct idiom is *obligation to*. "To" has an even greater advantage over "towards" in that context: it is shorter.

context = the whole, taking into account what goes before and comes after.

The boat is in the wrong context.

II

Interim Advice and Recommendations

The best way to good English is through authors whose worth is *established* by their classics. Good reference books — of which a dictionary is the most important — are also invaluable. Here is a short list of books I recommend. A more comprehensive list is at the end of this book.

DICTIONARIES

Oxford English Dictionary. Huge. The largest dictionary in the world. All central libraries in the English-speaking world have it. Examples the use of a word by eminent authors.

Shorter Oxford English Dictionary. Also examples how a word has been used.

Webster's New Twentieth Century Dictionary (Unabridged). American scholarship. Same size as the *Shorter Oxford*.

World Book Dictionary. American. Same size as the *Shorter Oxford*.

Chambers 20th Century Dictionary.

Longmans English Larousse. No longer published, but still in libraries. Of remarkable cultural value. Combines the essential features of dictionary and encyclopaedia. British & American scholarship under French control.

Oxford Illustrated Dictionary. Its illustrations are more technical than those of *Longmans English Larousse*.

---

classic = a work agreed by educated people to be in the best class
eminent = high above others
established = what is on a firm basis
Interim = in the meanwhile

The General Basic English Dictionary by C.K. Ogden. Explains 20,000 words using only 850 words.

Brewer's Dictionary of Phrase and Fable. "The most delightful of reference books." (The Times Literary Supplement)

GRAMMAR, VOCABULARY & STYLE

A.B.C. of English Usage by Treble & Vallins.

The Elements of Style by William Strunk & E.B. White. American.

The Facts of English by Ronald Ridout & Clifford Witting.

Outline of English Grammar by J.C. Nesfield.

Junior Course of English Composition by J.C. Nesfield.

Errors in English Composition by J.C. Nesfield.

Usage & Abusage by Eric Partridge.

The Oxford Miniguide To English Usage by E.S.C. Weiner.

The Complete Plain Words by Sir Ernest Gowers.

Dictionary of Modern English Usage by H.W. Fowler. (Revised by Ernest Gowers)

LITERATURE FOR CHILDREN AS WELL AS ADULTS

The Bible. Revised King James Version.

The Arthur Rackham Fairy Book. Published by George Harrap.

Aesop's Fables. Translated by F.C. Tilney. Published by J.M. Dent.

The Wind in the Willows by Kenneth Grahame.

Treasure Island by Robert Louis Stevenson.

Tom Sawyer, The Adventures of by Mark Twain.

Matilda by Roald Dahl

* * * *

Use no classic that is abridged ⑮

---

abridged = made shorter
translated = put in different words. (The Aesop was put into English from Greek)

III

Flabby English

VOCABULARY

Nothing, perhaps, is more characteristic of the flabbier kind of journalese than certain uses of *while*.

Fowler's Modern English Usage

while = at the *same time* as: during the *same time* that

Rugby from SABC News Bulletin

Transvaal won their match against the SA Police XV at Ellis Park in Johannesburg today by 36 points to 27. Robby Blair scored 20 points *while* Naas Botha scored 19 for the police team.

Correct that nonsense by putting *and* in place of *while*.

Other correctives of sentences that have misapplied 'whiles' are:

although = granting that: in spite of the fact that
whereas = when in fact

√	X
Although he promised not to do it, he did it.	*While* he promised not to do it, he did it. [If, however, he did the deed while he was promising, then the sense is right]
This rule applies only to licensed drivers, *but* (or *whereas*) he has no licence.	This rule applies only to licensed drivers, *while* he has no licence.

flabby = weak and ugly from soft fat
journalese = the language of bad journalism

STYLE

If you train your ear, tongue and eye to good English, your judgment will soon sharpen so that you are able to detect a poor thinker by his trashy English, and neither his expensive clothes nor his high position will turn you from correct judgment.

Here are examples of silly expressions that are frequent today. When these expressions were first used freshness gave some of them vitality, but now that they are stale, their combination of unoriginality and prolixity is doubly absurd. Except in rare contexts they are used nowadays by gas-bags who wish to sound important.

prolixity = too many words, or a long word instead of a better short one
stale = no good from age or over-use
vitality = liveliness

11

Gas-bag English	Meaning
alternative dentition	false teeth
at this moment (or point) in time	now
blue-print	plan
to dream up	to plan
expertise	skill
gunned down	shot dead
I am aware of	I know
I am conscious of	I know
The answer is in the affirmative	Yes
The answer is in the negative.	No
in-depth	thorough
engage in dialogue with	talk with
confrontation	argument; clash
economically viable	profitable
inferior extremities	feet
oral cavity	mouth
lower socio-economic group	the poor
master-minded	planned
lower-cost	cheaper
military hardware	arms
surgical evacuation	abortion
under-cover	secret

You may say, "But I've heard all those many times from people in high positions — even over radio and television!" The answer is: See that *you* don't use such rubbish.

IV

Brevity

You will have noticed from the last two pages that the better was the shorter.

The genius of English as of every other language, is towards accurate *brevity*. One unnecessary word wastes about half a second of a reader's time; if 100 000 people read it the collective waste is about 13 hours; but if a whole society of millions copies the long-windedness of inferior thinkers rather than the brevity of its best authors, that is even worse than a stupendous waste of time: it is a vast miscarriage of communal intelligence. Hesiod knew it when he said more than 2000 years ago: "He has mighty thanks who metes out each matter in a few words."

brevity = shortness
communal = shared by all the people
genius = the highest power for excellence
Hesiod: A poet of ancient Greece
metes = measures: limits
miscarriage = failure to reach a proper end
stupendous = amazingly large. From Latin *stupere* ... to be struck senseless (by amazement)
vast = of immense area or quantity

V

How to read a classic

Rules:

(9) (i) Have nothing to do with a classic that has been abridged or 'simplified' by an outsider, especially if it is for children: one of the reasons a classic has become a classic is that its author abridged and simplified it thoroughly.

(ii) Do not read what others, no matter how clever, have said about a classic, until you have read it and made your own judgment; then read the commentators.

(iii) If you do not know the meaning or pronunciation of a word go to a dictionary.

English has its particular sonance. Its great authors and orators are highly sensitive to its notes and rhythms. Therefore a classic must be *sounded*. This does not mean always reading aloud or even silently mouthing the words, but you should train your mind to hear the flow of fine language, and the pauses of its punctuation. Certainly, if you aim at a public career, reading aloud from first-class books should be a constant practice. Too many of today's public figures show in their platform utterances not only a stunted and inaccurate vocabulary, but insensitive ears. They are saved from failure, which would surely have been their lot a few generations ago, only by the matching ignorance and insensitivity of present mass audiences. Listen to a recording of a Churchill speech (public record libraries have collections) and you will hear real oratory. As to reading aloud, of another great orator, Abraham Lincoln, his business (49) partner wrote:

abridged = shortened
commentator = one who criticises or explains a thing
Lincoln, Abraham (1809 – 1863) 16th president of the USA. Campaigned against slavery.
orator = a public speaker of great eloquence
sonance = the quality of sound, especially from the voice. From Latin *sonare* ... to sound

"Mr Lincoln's habits, methods of reading law, politics, poetry, etc., etc., were to come into the office, pick up books, newspapers, etc., and to sprawl himself out on the sofa, chairs, etc., and read aloud, much to my annoyance. I have asked him often why he did so and his invariable reply was: 'I catch the idea by two senses, for when I read aloud I hear what is read and I see it; and hence two senses get it and I remember it better ...' "
ABRAHAM LINCOLN: HIS SPEECHES AND WRITINGS by Roy P. Basler. Page 47.

For Rule (iii) I suggest that you mark lightly in pencil the words to be looked up, and use the dictionary only when you have finished chapter, poem or scene. Unfolding of narrative or argument is thus not interrupted, and going back later may well bring to light more than you went back for: one of the remarkable things about a classic is that so many of its passages look better at a subsequent reading.

BBC Radio has a number of programmes illustrative of how English should be spoken. I particularly recommend *Letter From America*, *My Word* and *My Music*.

I also suggest you listen to good recordings of plays, novels and poetry. They can be got from a number of public libraries.

BBC = British Broadcasting Corporation

eloquence = the power of speaking with beauty and force that will persuade intelligent people

narrative = a recital of facts; a story; an account of. From Latin *gnarus* ... knowing – *narrare* ... to tell, to make known

subsequent = coming after, especially immediately after. From Latin *subsequi* ... to follow close after

VI

Punctuation

The main punctuations separate the thoughts of a writer, making their flow as clear as if he were speaking to you. They thus make reading as easy as listening. Always they indicate to the ear — a pause; and sometimes to the eye — the symmetry of the combined thoughts.

These main punctuations are:

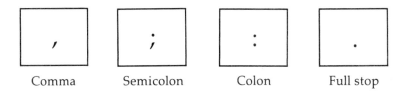

| Comma | Semicolon | Colon | Full stop |

They are called **stops** or **points**.

Comma: the shortest pause.
Semicolon: a pause slightly longer than that of the comma.
Colon: a pause slightly longer than that of the semicolon. Can also mean *as follows*.
Full stop: the longest pause.

Here they are in great literature:

Come now, and let us reason together, saith the Lord: though your sins be as scarlet, they shall be as white as snow; though they be red like crimson, they shall be as wool.

The Bible, Isaiah 1:18. Authorised King James Version.

---

pause = a short stop
punctuation = the division of sentences or words by points or other marks
symmetry = well-balanced arrangement of parts; harmony. From Greek *symmetria* ... right proportion

17

Now read that passage again, this time aloud, and use this little trick:

pause for one quick snap of your fingers for a comma,
pause for two quick snaps of your fingers for a semicolon,
pause for three quick snaps of your fingers for a colon, and
pause for four quick snaps of your fingers for a full stop.

Do that whenever you come to good writing whose punctuation is not at once clear to you, and your difficulty will be gone.

MORE ABOUT THE COMMA

A comma can be a boundary showing where one thought finishes and another begins. For example, the four thoughts of this multiple action

(i)   The drunken sot cursed his wife.
(ii)   Then he kicked the cat.
(iii) Then he tripped.
(iv)   Then he fell down the stairs.

are slotted together by commas thus:

The drunken sot cursed his wife, kicked the cat, tripped, and fell down the stairs.
    A comma can also be used to shorten a statement:

The first candidate was weak on grammar and the second candidate was strong on grammar.
The first candidate was weak on grammar, the second strong.

India beat Australia and Pakistan beat England.
India beat Australia, Pakistan England.

candidate = one who offers himself for a position of honour. From Latin *candidatus* ... clothed in white. (In ancient Rome it was the custom for candidates for office to present themselves in a white toga)
slotted = held together neatly, one part fitting into another
sot = one made stupid with drink
toga = In ancient Rome, the principal outer garment worn in public by citizens. It was a loose, flowing one-piece garment. It was the conventional town dress of the respectable man. From Latin *toga ... tangere ...* to cover

If you read the last pair of sentences aloud you will notice that in the longer sentence all the names are given equal stress, whereas in the shorter one India and Pakistan are strongly stressed. To put it another way – that sort of comma forces you to attend carefully to the beginning of the statement, and your extra attention is shown by the tone of your voice. The same rule of sound applies to the first pair. And you need not think of the rule: your ear will immediately put you on the right stress.

The three main mistakes with commas are to leave them out, to put them in, and to misplace them.

Wrongly left out

X	√
Zeus came to her in the tower where her father kept her locked up in the form of a shower of gold.	Zeus came to her in the tower where her father kept her locked up, in the form of a shower of gold.

The comma on the right side shows that Zeus, not the girl, was in the form of a shower of gold. If you would rather have the girl in the form of a shower of gold, remove the comma.

X	√
A lictor was an officer of ancient Rome whose functions were to attend upon a magistrate bearing the fasces.	A lictor was an officer of ancient Rome whose functions were to attend upon a magistrate, bearing the fasces.

fasces: a bundle of wooden rods with an axe in the middle with its head projecting. It was the symbol of a Roman magistrate's authority
stress = force of breath put onto something said, to make it more noticeable
Zeus = was the supreme god of the ancient Greeks

Without the comma it would have been the magistrate bearing the fasces.

A valise is a large waterproof case for an officer's bedding and spare clothing rolled up from one end and secured by straps.	A valise is a large waterproof case for an officer's bedding and spare clothing, rolled up from one end and secured by straps.

The comma shows that 'rolled up' applies to 'valise'. In the sentence without the comma it is only the 'spare clothing' that is rolled up from one end and secured by straps.

Those last three sentences under the correct tick show the 'throwing back' power of a comma — its signal that what comes *after* it must be applied to the *beginning* of the statement.

Now see how the leaving out of commas can turn sense into nonsense.

President Reagan says Associated Press is suffering from cancer.	President Reagan, says Associated Press, is suffering from cancer.
President Reagan does the saying, and says that Associated Press has cancer.	Associated Press says that President Reagan has cancer.

Wrongly put in

Men, who have poor eyesight, make poor pilots.	Men who have poor eyesight make poor pilots.
[Applies to *all* men, which is a nonsense.]	[Applies only to men with bad eyesight.]

20

| The boys, sang beautifully. They left, after the concert. | The boys sang beautifully. They left after the concert. |

[Those commas have less logic than a hiccup. Grammatical reason against them will be given later. In the meantime see and *hear* for yourself that they stop the flow of straight-forward statements.]

Misplaced

| The drunken sot cursed, his wife kicked the cat, tripped, and fell down the stairs. | The drunken sot cursed his wife, kicked the cat, tripped, and fell down the stairs. |

| I ordered butter, cheese and, eggs. | I ordered butter, cheese, and eggs. |

Again, it should be apparent from sound and sight that a comma after 'and' in such a sentence is wrong.

| He saw that many, if not most of, the dancers were bare-footed. | He saw that many, if not most, of the dancers were bare-footed. |

The main part of that sentence is 'He saw that many of the dancers were bare-footed'. 'If not most', is subsidiary to it.

subsidiary = of secondary importance. From Latin *sub* ... under & *sedere* ... to sit

21

The comma after *of* spoils the form of the sentence.

| While the enemy's attack was at its height and seemed certain to succeed, the surviving machine-gunners, instead of retreating heroically, ran forward to the knoll. | While the enemy's attack was at its height and seemed certain to succeed, the surviving machine-gunners, instead of retreating, heroically ran forward to the knoll. |

SEMICOLON

As you saw earlier, it is a stronger stop than the comma; its pause is longer. It shows that the thoughts on either side of it are closely connected and should be weighed against each other. To the eye it indicates form; to the ear, stress.

COLON

It can add vigour to statements by strongly marking them both in sight and in sound:

But such men as Howe and Seymour hated him implacably: they hated his commanding genius much: they hated the mild majesty of his virtue still more.

Macaulay's HISTORY OF ENGLAND

It can also be the strongest marker of antithesis or other balance. It does this by showing itself immediately to the reader as the pivot of the contrast or the similarity:

antithesis = a contrast of dissimilars or direct opposites. From Greek *anti* ... against + *tithenai* ... to place
form = shape
implacably = which nothing will make less (of anger, hate); not to be placated. From Latin *im* ... not + *placare* ... to take away anger
knoll = little hill
majesty = in the manner of a very high ruler such as a king, queen, or God
pivot = a point on which anything (such as a scale) turns
vigour = lively strength. From Latin *vigere* ... to be strong

A fool uttereth all his mind: but a wise man keepeth it in till afterwards. BIBLE (King James) Proverbs

The legs of the lame are not equal: so is a parable in the mouth of fools. Ib.

In its most general modern application it says "as follows", as in the introductions to my examples of it, and in announcements of lists:

Please send the following:

> 100 spark-plugs
> 45 carburettors
> 2 crankshafts

FULL STOP

Called *period* by Americans.

It is the strongest stop. It signals "that thought is ended", and, when between words – "that thought is ended. Now starts the next thought".

And the next thought always starts with a capital letter. Sir Ernest Gowers in THE COMPLETE PLAIN WORDS states the rule:

"Always use a full stop to separate statements between which there is no continuity of thought."

√	X
Ice hockey is a dangerous game. Last year our team had twelve injuries.	Ice hockey is a dangerous game, last year our team had twelve injuries.

Ib. is short for Latin *ibidem* . . . in the same place
parable = proverb = a short story full of wisdom. It teaches some moral lesson
uttereth = speaks

X

A colon instead of a full stop between the statements would also be correct, but it would give a different shade of meaning by signalling a continuity of thought.	Ice hockey is a dangerous game and last year our team had twelve injuries.

The rest of the punctuations are:

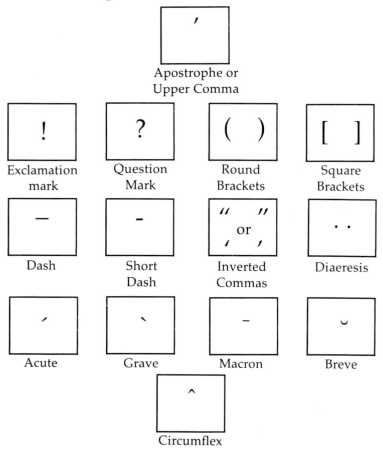

Apostrophe or
Upper Comma

Exclamation
mark

Question
Mark

Round
Brackets

Square
Brackets

Dash

Short
Dash

Inverted
Commas

Diaeresis

Acute

Grave

Macron

Breve

Circumflex

There are two apostrophes for punctuation.

(i) THE POSSESSIVE APOSTROPHE

It is not a stop. Its main function is to indicate possession, which it does in indissoluble partnership with *s*. That partnership stands for *of*.

Singular

The boss's coat	=	The coat of the boss
John's coat	=	The coat of John
Charles's coat	=	The coat of Charles
Burns's coat	=	The coat of Burns
Dickens's coat	=	The coat of Dickens
Keats's coat	=	The coat of Keats
Jones's coat	=	The coat of Jones
The man's coat	=	The coat of the man
The boy's coat	=	The coat of the boy
The girl's coat	=	The coat of the girl
The child's coat	=	The coat of the child
The princess's coat	=	The coat of the princess
The MP's coat	=	The coat of the MP
Everybody's coat	=	The coat of each (person)
One's coat	=	The coat of one (person)
Anybody's coat	=	The coat of any (person)
The ox's coat	=	The coat of the ox
The sheep's coat	=	The coat of the sheep

Plural

The bosses' coats	=	The coats of the bosses
The Burnses' coats	=	The coats of the Burnses
The Dickenses' coats	=	The coats of the Dickenses

function = a special action of one thing that influences something else. From Latin *fungi* ... to perform
indissoluble = that cannot be separated. From Latin *in* ... not & *dissolvere* ... to loosen
plural = more than one person or thing
singular = one person or thing

The Keatses' coats	=	The coats of the Keatses
The Joneses' coats	=	The coats of the Joneses
The men's coats	=	The coats of the men
The boys' coats	=	The coats of the boys
The girls' coats	=	The coats of the girls
The children's coats	=	The coats of the children
The princesses' coats	=	The coats of the princesses
The MPs' coats	=	The coats of the MPs
The oxen's coats	=	The coats of the oxen
The sheep's coats	=	The coats of the sheep

Rules for those apostrophes

*There must be an **s** with the apostrophe*

In singular the apostrophe is always on the left of its s; in plural it is generally on the right, the plural word supplying the necessary s from its ending (two boys').

The possessive apostrophe always follows the completed word.

That means that a possessive apostrophe should never split a word: do not split Jones' into Jone's, princesses into princesse's. Always make it clear that the extra s, i.e. the apostrophe s is not made part of the word (*oxen* is a word, *oxens'* is not).

One of the things that frustrate foreigners learning English is the exception to rule that English frequently presents. This natural tendency of English to go around rules when they get in the way has probably, especially amongst nations used to a more rigid conformity in their own languages, contributed to the sentiment behind the old political curse 'Perfidious Albion!'. But these exceptions should not be taken as signs that English-speakers are more prone to insincerity than speakers of other tongues. It is just that English has special problems because of its hybrid nature and enormous vocabulary. Some of these problems will be presented later.

Albion is an old name for England, perhaps from the white cliffs of England facing France. From Latin *albus* ... white
hybrid = made up of very different parts
Perfidious = being false to friends. From Latin *perfidus* ... treacherous
prone = having a tendency to bend downwards towards. From Latin *pronus* ... *towards*

Exceptions to the Possessive Apostrophe Rules
(They are very few)

Classical singulars like Zeus, Mars, Venus; Hebrew ones like Moses, Jesus:

Zeus' coat
Mars' coat
Venus' coat
Moses' coat
Jesus' coat or Jesu's coat
(*Jesu*, derived from the Greek, was the regular name until after 1500, when the Latin *Jesus* became the regular. *Jesu* is still frequent)

The possessives *yours*, *theirs*, *its*, *hers*, *ours* and *his* never have (28) an apostrophe:

its coat
The coat is yours, hers, his
The coats are theirs, ours

In the idiomatic phrases:

for conscience' sake   =   for the sake of conscience
for goodness' sake   =   for the sake of goodness

The classical and Hebrew exceptions can always be avoided by writing:

The coat of Jesus
The coat of Zeus, etc.

Classical = from ancient Greece and Rome. From Latin *classicus* ... of the highest class   (8)
etc. is short for Latin *et cetera* = and the rest
Mars = The Roman god of war
Venus = The Roman goddess of beauty and sexual love

(ii) The Other Apostrophe

In this use it signals that something has been left out:

on't	=	on it
don't	=	do not
can't	=	cannot
o'er	=	over
e'er	=	ever
it's	=	it is, or it has (It's been raining)

(Do not confuse with possessive *its*) (27)

(iii) Another Apostrophe

I blush at having to announce yet another apostrophe. These three have been loose in English for hundreds of years. This last one has nothing to do with punctuation, but it had better be mentioned here for the sake of completion, and as a warning example of how ill-applied terms can be kept in circulation to the lasting detriment of precision. Certainly, in such a specialized field as technical terminology for the English language, to call three very different operations by the same name is a blunder in nomenclature. Fortunately such blunders are rare from grammarians of the past.

In this third sense *apostrophe* is a technical term in rhetoric. It is 'a turning aside from the course of a speech or writing in order to make a short address to a person or thing, whether present or absent'. For example, Hamlet, distraught with his mother's re-marrying indecently-soon after his beloved father's death, breaks off his soliloquy to address Frailty:

Must I remember? Why, she would hang on him
As if increase of appetite had grown

---

detriment = damage, loss. From Latin *deterere* ... to wear away
distraught = almost off one's head with trouble. From Latin *distrahere* ... to drag apart
frailty = readily giving way to wrong impulses through weakness. From Latin *fragilis* ...
　easily broken.
nomenclature = system of giving names. From Latin *nomen* ... name + *calare* ... to call
rhetoric = the art or science of persuading through language. From Greek *rhetorika* Latin
　rhetorica ... the rhetorical art
soliloquy = a speech to oneself. From Latin *solus* ... alone + *loqui* ... speak

By what it fed on; and yet within a month!
Let me not think on't. Frailty, thy name is woman.

HAMLET I-ii-146

The unsuitability of the term *apostrophe* is in inverse proportion to the importance of its three uses. For possession, its commonest and most important use, it is most unfitting. How, asks the intelligent learner, can 'James's coat' be connected with the etymology of *apostrophe* which is *a turning away*? Nor can the term be logically squared with 'omission' even after one has dug down to Anglo-Saxon and seen the logical ground for the sign. Only in rhetoric, its rarest application, can one see at once from the Greek meaning of *apostrophe* ... a turning away to a particular person or thing, that the term fits.

I suggest the following tags: *possessive-upper comma* for possessive apostrophe, *omission-upper-comma* for omission apostrophe, *apostrophe* for its rhetorical use.

EXCLAMATION MARK:

A full stop or comma, expressing strong emotion or strong command. Think of it as steam rising from a full stop or comma: "Help!" "I love you!" "Come here!" "Look out!" Use sparingly: it can be hysterical, like the dash.

QUESTION MARK:

Sign of a *direct* question. It is a full stop and is therefore followed by a capital letter, except in constructions such as "How old are you?" he asked.

Not to be used in such as: *He asked how old I was.* That is not a *direct* question. It is a statement.

Anglo-Saxon = the Old English language spoken in England between 450 and 1100
capital = chief. A B C D are capitals of a b c d. From Latin *capitalis* ... chief; most important
etymology = a description of the path by which a word has come to its meaning and spelling. It is the history of a word from its origin. From Greek *etymon* ... the original sense or form of a word
tags = labels

ROUND BRACKETS

enclose less important comments or explanations. What is within them should be so subsidiary to the statement outside them that its removal would leave no gap either in sense or in punctuation:

I am told that the mayor's speech (which my wife and I could not hear) was boring.

Three rules:

(i) Brackets must always be in pairs.

(ii) A full stop is the only punctuation that can appear immediately before the first bracket. In other words, there should be no punctuation immediately before the first bracket (full stop excepted).

(iii) There should be no punctuation immediately after the closing bracket, unless the punctuation belonged to the main statement, i.e. would be correct there if the bracketed remark were removed:

I knocked frantically on the door (my bruised hands are still paining), but received no answer.

Zeus came to her in the tower where her father kept her locked up (Danaë was her name), in the form of a shower of gold.

SQUARE BRACKETS

indicate that the remark they enclose is even less related to a main statement than a remark in round brackets. Such a remark is usually put in by someone other than the writer of the main statement:

Napoleon died on Elba [wrong again!] in 1821.
They can also be used within round brackets:
Napoleon died on Elba (I think it was Elba [think again!]) in 1821.
Same rules as for round brackets.

THE DASH

suddenly stops the flow of thought, either to hold the reader in suspense, or to put another thought to him before resuming the original one. Suspense:

I saw his mad eyes glitter as he raised the stick, saw the first part of its descent, and then saw — flashing lights and stars.

Thought sandwiched:

Soldiers! If we win this battle — and who can doubt that we shall not? — we need fight no more.

(29) Because the dash is such an arresting stop it should be used sparingly, else it gives an air of ineffectual excitability.

You saw from the last example that dashes can act like brackets. If so used, they must conform to the three bracket rules.

The dash has three more uses:

(i) To indicate a sudden turn away:
   "Now I'll show you my most valuable possession, the diamond necklace my husband —— It's gone, it's gone, it's been stolen!"
(ii) To show hesitancy or uncertainty:
   "He — er — said — no — I can't remember what he said."
(iii) To put an announcement into order:
   "Here on the platform are three atrocious murderers in wax — Bluebeard, George Joseph Smith (the modern Bluebeard), and Heinrich Himmler."

SHORT DASH (called Hyphen)

is the opposite of the dash:

The dash separates, the hyphen joins — and it joins only *within* words. For examples, *father-in-law, battle-field, common-sense,*

arresting = holds you strongly. From Latin *ad* ... to + *restare* ... stay back
descent = the coming down. From Latin *de* ... down from + *scandere* ... to climb
resuming = taking up again. From Latin *re* ... again + *sumere* ... to take
suspense = an anxious state of doubt. From Latin *suspensus* ... hanging, uncertain

and that never-to-be-forgotten compound of Ben Jonsons's *un-in-one-breath-utterable* — each should be thought of as one word.

The dash requires no careful thought of a writer, but the hyphen does because its being in or out or misplaced can make a great difference in such as:

She was a light-house keeper's daughter.

She was a light house-keeper's daughter.

Heading
Hang-glider pilots!

Heading
Hang glider pilots!

For those two gems I am endebted to W.J. Weston in THE MANUAL OF GOOD ENGLISH, and Gerald Zwirn in the Johannesburg STAR respectively.

He has a big loud-speaker.

He has a big loud speaker.
[Fat wife?]

Those twenty-odd people are my friends.

Those twenty odd people are my friends.

---

compound = a bigger thing made from joining together smaller things. From Latin
   componere ... to put together
i.e. is short for Latin *id est* ... that is
inverted = turned upside down. From Latin *invertere* ... turned the opposite way
odd. In the examples it has two meanings;
   i. not matching; not normal; strange; eccentric
   ii. a few more than
twenty odd people = twenty strange people
twenty-odd people = a few more than twenty people
quotation = a saying again; a repeat
syllable = a single sounding in language, i.e. a vowel with one or more consonants. Hell,
   death, like, love, all have one syllable
   In butter there are two syllables, in divided three ... butt er   div i ded

In speech the signal for a hyphenated word is a heavy stress (a thump) on the syllable before the first short dash.

> The differences between
> *re-cover* and *recover*
> *re-pair* and *repair*
> *twenty-odd* and *twenty odd*

are heard immediately.

Other uses of the hyphen such as its making a join in a word that must be continued to the next line, and its indication of stuttering (D-d-d-don't g-g-g-go) —— I leave to your observation and common-sense.

INVERTED COMMAS (or Quotation Marks)

"Do you mean that you think you can find out the answer to it?" said the March Hare.

"Exactly so," said Alice.

"Then you should say what you mean."

"I do," Alice hastily replied, "at least — at least I mean what I say — that's the same thing, you know."

"Not the same thing a bit!" said the Hatter. "Why, you might just as well say that 'I see what I eat' is the same as 'I eat what I see'!"

(*Alice in Wonderland*)

You see either "___" or '___' is correct. That passage could have started

'Do you mean...?', and punctuated the Hatter *'Why, you might just as well say that "I see what I eat" is the same as "I eat what I see"!'*

The rule that applies here is so obvious as hardly to need stating: quotation marks must, like brackets, be always in pairs; and *pairs* here means 'exact pair'; "___' is lopsidedly wrong.

The main rule for quotation marks is that they must enclose the actual words of a speaker or passage quoted.

X

He said, "It is bad mannered   He said, "It was bad manne-
of you not to rise in greeting   red of me not to rise in greet-
an elder."   ing an elder."

He said it was bad mannered of me not to rise in greeting an elder.

Inverted commas can also be used to highlight words (as with
'exact pair' above), and to show irony or contempt:

It [sociology] is therefore an attempt to define 'experimentally'
the laws of evolution of human society in such a way as to
'predict' that the oak tree will develop out of the acorn.
                        (*Antonio Gramsci* PRISON NOTEBOOKS)

Quotation marks are a modern addition to English. They are
really not necessary. The Bible does well enough without them,
and so do many other classics.

comprehends = takes in completely. From Latin *comprehendere* ... to catch hold of all
  together.
individual = a single person as contrasted to Society, Group or Crowd. An individual
  must be thought of as a separate, special person. From Latin *individuus* ... not divisible
scientific = in the manner of science. Science is the *best method* of gathering and dealing
  with knowledge. There is only one Science. Its various classes can be thought of as
  different rooms in the same house. Scientific method reasons *only from facts*. It depends
  upon i. Intelligent collection and ordering of facts and ii. Nomenclature that enables the
  facts to be worked with the utmost economy of effort and time
    Science and Capitalism are alike in that Capitalism uses money to get more money,
  and Science uses facts to get more facts. However, whereas there is bad capitalism, there
  is no bad science —— if it's bad it's not Science. From Latin *scire* ... to know
sociology is the study of causes and effects of the pressures of a society on its individuals,
  with a view to solving social problems. The study aims at being scientific, to the extent
  of arriving at generalizations and scientific laws, and it comprehends origin, develop-
  ment and present state of the institutions of society. No study could be vaster or more
  important, and it deserves the best brains and wisest gathering of experience but, alas,
  the great majority of its teachers and students are intellectually insufficient

DIAERESIS

The two dots placed over the second of two consecutive vowels show that that second vowel is also pronounced. Germans call it an *umlaut*: Noël Coward, Chloë, aërate, coördinate. It is more common in American usage than in British. Coördinate and coöperate in British usage are co-ordinate and co-operate.

THE ACUTE AND THE GRAVE

are primarily French signs, common in French but rare in English. They are emphasizers to show stress on a vowel. Acute indicates strong stress, and grave a weaker stress. Émigré, café, cliché, communiqué, élite, exposé, début, débris, résumé are acutely stressed. The present trend in English is not to use accent marks. Take your choice, but be consistent: if you show one accent do not leave the others out.

√   X

résumé   résume

The grave shows stress on a vowel, but stress weaker than that of an acute. For example, the first syllable of *typewriter* is more strongly stressed than the second syllable, and this can be shown by acute and grave so, *týpewrìter*. If you say it you will automatically give it the right stresses (if you are English-speaking), and if you pay attention to pitch you will notice that your tone of voice for the strongly stressed *type* was higher than for the weakly stressed *writer*.

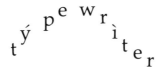

acute = sharp, severe. From Latin *actus* ... sharp, from *acus* ... needle
(1) **consecutive** = following uninterrupted in order. It has the notion of "nearness". 1, 2, 3, 4, 5 are consecutive. From Latin *consequi* ... to follow closely
grave = weighty. From French *grave* ... deep-voiced. To French from Latin *gravis* ... heavy
pitch = highness or lowness of a note. A canary has a higher pitched voice than a bull
sonorous = full of sound. From Latin *sonorus* ... full of sound
vowels = the only sonorous sounds of language. They are made in the throat. A E I O U are the vowels of English. From Latin *vocalis* ... singing

The grave invariably shows a falling pitch [discothèque]. It is used with the acute in scansion of verse to show the rhythm of a line:

To bé, or nót to bè: thát is the quéstion:

(HAMLET Act III Scene I)

The rhythm of English poetry is made by these alternate strong and weak stresses that are as posts between unstressed syllables. The strong stress, as well as being higher in pitch, is also louder than the weak stress, and these ever-varying pitches and volumes are vital to the sound and *sense* of good English.

The grave is also put over an *e* that is normally not sounded, as a sign that it must be pronounced, usually for the rhythm of verse:

> His mother was a learnèd lady, famed
> For every branch of every science known,
> In every Christian language ever named,
> With virtues equalled by her wit alone.
>
> (Byron's DON JUAN, Canto I, x)

> Why art thou yet so fair? Shall I believe
> That unsubstantial Death is amorous,
> And that the lean abhorrèd monster keeps
> Thee here in dark to be his paramour?
>
> (Shakespeare's ROMEO & JULIET Act V, Scene iii)

O cursèd were the cruel wars that ever they should rise
And out of merry England press many a lad likewise!

(HIGH GERMANY, Anonymous)

---

paramour = a sweetheart; an unlawful sexual lover. From French *par amour* ... through sexual love. To French from Latin *per* ... by + *amor* ... love

press = to force a man to serve in the army or navy; to conscript

scansion = the analysis of verse into its rhythmic parts. From Latin *scandere* ... to climb (from keeping time with the feet in music). "To scan" in English means to look *most carefully*

THE MACRON AND THE BREVE

They have two different employments, one in pronunciation, the other in scansion of verse.

In pronunciation the macron indicates long sound for a vowel, and the breve short sound: Ē (bee) Ĕ (hen) Ō (oh) Ŏ (bob) Ā (ay) Ă (cab) Rōman, făscēs

Here they are convenient guides for those English-speakers (a majority) who have not mastered more complicated phonetic systems such as IPA (International Phonetic Alphabet).

In verse scansion they can be used instead of acute and grave, the ⁻ taking the place of ´, and the ˘ taking the place of ` to illustrate the most simple mechanics of English poetry:
Tŏ bē, ŏr nŏt tŏ bē: that ĭs thē quēstiōn:

My main purpose in assigning macron, breve, acute and grave to Punctuation is to make an easy opening to English poetry for deprived adults who have never been touched by poetry in their childhood homes, and who were alienated from it at school by inept teachers. Of course, in presenting poetry to children such mechanics should not even be mentioned until the children have been imbued with poetry through listening to it from an early age. A normal child of six, without any knowledge of scansion, will be deeply moved by a straightforward rendering of the poem which begins with the famous lines:

> *The boy stood on the burning deck*
> *Whence all but he had fled ...*

---

alienated = turned away from because it is made unpleasing. From Latin *alienare* ... to keep apart from by making it strange.

breve = that which makes short. French *breve* ... short, brief. From Latin *brevis*.

convenient = making things easier. From Latin *convenient* ... was suitable

imbued = become used to it by being soaked in it. From Latin *imbuere* ... to stain by soaking.

inept = clumsy. From Latin *ineptus* ... stupid; clumsy.

Macron = that which makes long. French *macron* from Greek *makros* ... long.

verse = the rhythm of poetry. Not all verse is poetry. In order to become poetry the verse must carry deep feeling, deep thought.

But obtrude pedantry before love of poetry has taken root and you will almost certainly extinguish a divine light of childhood.

CIRCUMFLEX

Comes to English from French. It indicates a rise *and* fall of pitch in the vowel over which it bends: its pronunciation is started on a rising pitch and midway the pitch is lowered. Nowadays its use is optional in English. The same rule applies to it as to the acute and grave: if you put one accent in you must put them all in.

√	X
mêlée	melée
tête-à-tête	tête-a-tête

*   *   *   *   *   *   *   *   *

I am indebted to my old schoolmaster, Mr R. Coldrey, for the following problem which he recently gave me with its solution. For fun try to punctuate sense into:

that that is is that that is not is not
is not that so it is (Solution is at bottom of page 40)

*   *   *   *

Vocabulary

But signals opposition or contrast. When there is no sense of either do not use *but*.

√	X
John bought an ice-cream, *and* Joseph bought a hamburger.	John bought an ice-cream, *but* Joseph bought a hamburger.

circumflex = bend round. From Latin *circumflexus* ... bent around
obtrude = to press (a matter, person, etc.) on others unwanted. From Latin *obtrudere* ... to thrust or press upon
optional = giving one the power to select freely for oneself
pedantry = teaching that over-values rules and misses the beauty. From French *pedant* ... an inept teacher

He was not affected by the wine; what made him drunk was the beer. [The logic of punctuation!]	He was not affected by the wine, *but* what made him drunk was the beer.

Between & Among: When *sharing* is thought of, *between* is for two, *among* (or amongst) for more than two.

The money was divided *among* the three thieves.	The money was divided *between* the three thieves.
The cake was shared *between* the two of us.	The cake was shared *among* the two of us.

When, however, there is no thought of *sharing,* "between" is used even when there are three or more.

After much wrangling there was agreement *between* the ten politicians.	After much wrangling there was agreement *among* the ten politicians.
If I had to choose *between* Joseph, Peter and Paul, I should choose Paul.	If I had to choose *among* Joseph, Peter and Paul, I should choose Paul.

wrangling = noisy, peevish dispute

39

Verbal = in words. From Latin *verbum* ... a word
Oral = in spoken words. From Latin *oris* ... mouth

Mr Coetzee was giving *verbal* evidence in Cape town. [He spoke it] SABC Radio News

Oral would have been better in that context.

Solution

"That that is, is. That that is not, is not. Is not that so?"
   "It is".

VII

Metaphor & Simile

Metaphor

We all naturally find it agreeable to get hold of new ideas immediately ... It is from metaphor that we can best get hold of something fresh.

A good writer or speaker is master of many things in language for making his ideas lively and memorable. But the greatest thing by far is to be a master of metaphor. It is the one thing that cannot be learnt from others; and it is also a sign of genius, since a good metaphor implies an intuitive perception of the similarity in dissimilars.

That, except for a few bridging words of mine, is pure Aristotle (from his RHETORIC, Book III and POETICS, Chapter 22).

Metaphor	Literal
A withered stalk	Old age

Robert Louis Stevenson writing of a very old man who had held high office (MEMORIES AND PORTRAITS)

You could not say that he
had lost his memory, for he
would repeat Shakespeare
and Webster and Jeremy

Aristotle (384 B.C. – 322 B.C.) Greek philosopher

literal = words in their straightforward sense

metaphor = a name or quality put to something to which it is not really (literally) applicable, and so it implies a likeness between two things on a special point, e.g. *nerves of steel* = strong nerves. Latin *metaphora* = transfer

simile = a direct pointing at a likeness between two things. From Latin *similis* ... like

Webster, John (c. 1580 – c. 1625) Jacobean dramatist. His work was at first not popular, and he expressed contempt for the 'uncapable multitude', and wished to be read in the light of such as Ben Jonson and Shakespeare, whom he knew personally. His wish has been fulfilled by two of his plays, THE WHITE DEVIL and THE DUCHESS OF MALFI being classed with the great tragedies of English

Metaphor	Literal
Taylor and Burke by the page together; but the parchment was filled up, there was no room for fresh inscriptions, and he was capable of repeating the same anecdote on many successive visits	parchment = memory of the old man inscriptions = deep impressions
Most doors can be opened with a golden key	doors = obstacles golden key = money Money has tremendous influence
:keep the doors of thy mouth from her that lieth in thy bosom (BIBLE Micah 7:5)	doors of thy mouth = silence, prudence Do not blab to the woman you love
Gave up my *fort of silence* to a woman	silence as prudence for safety

Samson, after his eyes were put out, bewailing his silliness in blabbing out his secret to Dalila (SAMSON AGONISTES by John Milton)

---

blab = foolishly let out secrets in talk

Burke, Edmund (1729 – 1797) British statesman in the House of Commons. Eminent orator.

fort = a place made strong so that soldiers can hold out against a more numerous enemy. From Latin *fortis* ... strong

inscriptions = writings intended to last. Done on surfaces such as stone, coins, parchment. From Latin *in* ... into + *scribere* ... to write

parchment = animal skin prepared as a writing surface. Only writing worth preserving would be inscribed on it

prudence = taking care for the future; acting only after thinking. From Latin *prudentia* ... prudence

Taylor, Jeremy (1613 – 1667) Anglican bishop. His sermons are masterpieces of 17th-century prose

tremendous = so great as to make one tremble. From Latin *tremere* ... to tremble

Metaphor	Literal
Mercy and truth are met together; righteousness and peace have kissed each other (Bible Psalm 35:10)	Mercy & truth make for a righteous peace
Vain the ambition of kings Who seek by trophies and dead things To leave a living name behind, *And weave but nets to catch the wind.* (John Webster)	Such action is utterly ineffectual
He that loves not his wife and children, *feeds a lioness at home, and broods a nest of sorrows.* (Jeremy Taylor – THE MARRIAGE RING	makes his wife dangerously fierce, and makes increasing sorrows for the whole family
Example is the school of mankind, and they will learn at no other. (Edmund Burke)	Mankind learns only from example
When we speak of 'morality in progress,' we mean the maintenance by man of his control of the situation — to our highest concept of what is right between man and man — and not merely consent to be *moulded out of moral shape by the pressure of progress* Henry Ford – MY PHILOSOPHY OF INDUSTRY	act in a weak and morally worse way because of material progress

How flat the literal is next to the metaphorical! Aristotle gives the reason:

"People are not much taken either by obvious arguments (using the word 'obvious' to mean what is plain to everybody and needs no investigation), nor by those which puzzle us ... but only by those which convey their information to us as soon as we hear them." (RHETORIC, Book III)

Simile

If metaphor is the diamond of style, simile is its gold. Simile is really metaphor lengthened by "like" or "as", and it ranks below metaphor because it is longer.

red as a beetroot

---

as good as gold

You could liken his face to a lemon gone bad

... this knowledge [of Truth] must continually be renewed by ceaseless effort, if it is not to be lost. *It resembles a statue of marble which stands in the desert and is continuously threatened with burial by the shifting sand.*
(Albert Einstein ON EDUCATION from OUT OF MY LATER YEARS)

But beware of simile and metaphor. They immediately show a user's brightness, dullness or stupidity. They have three levels:

flat = having no surprises, no sparkle

hilltops, middle-ground, and bog. They sparkle on the hilltops, are dull on the middle-ground of cliché, and are ludicrous in the bog. All the previous examples were from the hilltops. Here are some from the middle-ground of cliché:

64 000 dollar question	=	the main question
iron out the problem	=	solve the problem
the sporting fraternity	=	sportsmen
writing on the wall	=	dire warning
tiny tots	=	infants
staff of life	=	bread
as good as gold	=	excellently well behaved

Why is the last one on that list when only a short while back it was listed 'hilltop'? The answer is that each of the middle-grounders was excellent when it was used by its creator, but became outworn through too much use by others. If you were to use any of the sparklers I have recorded, you would degrade them to the middle-ground, *if you were writing seriously*. In informal writing or light conversation most of us use cliché-metaphor, but then such writing or speaking does not take us to the hilltops.

☐ From the bog:

☐ An Irish politician in the House of Commons two hundred years ago ____

"Mr Speaker, I *smell a rat*. I see it floating in the air; and if it is not *nipped in the bud*, it will burst forth into a terrible *conflagration* that will deluge the world."

That is probably the most famous mixed metaphor bag in English. A metaphor is mixed when it puts incongruous com-

---

bog = low ground that, because of poor drainage, is permanently under water, mud and rotten vegetation

conflagration = a great, destructive fire. From Latin *conflagare* ... to burn very much

deluge = violent rainfall that causes a great flood. From Latin *dis* = off + *lavere* ... to wash

House of Commons: the assembly of elected representatives in the British parliament

incongruous = having parts that do not fit together; out of harmony. From Latin *in* ... not + *congruere* ... to come together.

nipped : a nip is a small, quick, sharp bite

parisons on an object in quick succession — — — a rat floating in the air is incongruous enough, but its being nipped in the bud (a metaphor that calls up the idea of a flower being killed in the first stage of its growth), and then turning into a huge destructive fire that will flood (drown) the world — — — that is a memorable stew.

Rule: Do not mix two metaphors so that they clash on the same object.

In the following examples the metaphors are not mixed, just incongruous.

An Italian writing to an English publisher:

"The thought that I have *sown and manured* for six months has at last *flowered* into a concrete proposal."

A sports-master:

"And now I speak to the rugby team. Boys will be boys, and high spirits are all very well, but when I find that tacks have been scattered over the changeroom floor I, as your trainer, must *put my foot down.*"

A medical doctor speaking over SABC Radio as spokesman for hospitals ___

"... are going to handle accident situations *on a top basis.*"

Quite apart from its general flabbiness, that's a howler because, in putting "top" with "basis" it awakens the dormant knowledge of an educated person and reminds him that "basis" comes from *base* = bottom, and the idea of top/bottom with the extra connotations of "handle", and the "sit" of "situations" flashes an irresistible picture to the normally lavatorial English-speaking mind. The meaning aimed at was, I guess, "... will treat casualties promptly."

Three General Rules for simile and metaphor:

(i) Even if you have a good stock of original ones, be sparing

---

dormant = lying asleep. From Latin *dormire* ... to sleep
howler = a mistake from ignorance that makes people howl with laughter
lavatorial = to do with a lavatory. Lavatory = a place that takes human body-waste and then washes it away into a sewer; a toilet. *From Latin lavare* ... to wash
stew = a mixture of meat and several vegetables slowly boiled; a state of confusion and great alarm

with them: generally they make their point in isolation, and are blunted when packed closely together.

(ii) Prepare the way for a metaphor (simile can do with less preparation) so that it comes as the final and brightest illumination. See how well Stevenson prepared you for his "parchment" metaphor.

(iii) For serious communication prefer plain unmetaphorical to overworked figures of speech:

We can be proud	rather than	We can hold our heads high
do our best	rather than	put our best foot forward
tell the secrets	rather than	spill the beans
firmly disallow	rather than	put our foot down
gradually stopped	rather than	ground to a halt
very well behaved	rather than	good as gold

But worn simile and metaphor are now so numerous and deep into everyday English that, like lines of potholes across a teeming motorway, they are avoided only by careful attention. The rewards of such attention will be heightened sensibility and more powerful expression that on occasion may even supply you with your very own figures of speech for influencing people.

As to the magnitude of metaphor in influencing people to turn great events, history gives examples, but none that I know is more striking than this one. The story is told in FORTRESS WITHOUT A ROOF: THE ALLIED BOMBING OF THE THIRD REICH by Wilbur H. Morrison.

In 1942 the Americans and the British were in deep disagreement over their main war effort, the air bombing from England of Germany and German-occupied Europe.

---

isolation = kept apart from others (metaphors). From Latin *insula* . . . an island

numerous = in large numbers; many. From Latin *numerus* . . . number

occasion = the right time from good luck giving one a special opportunity; also – a special time. From Latin *occasio* . . . accidental opportunity

sensibility = quickness and power to perceive and to feel emotion; power of delicate feeling, especially for beauty. From Latin *sensibilis* . . . sensible

The British bombed only at night, the Americans only by day, and the British wanted the Americans to give up daylight bombing for night bombing. The Americans were adamant not to change.

The arguments for and against either stand are too long and complex for this short book whose subject is far removed from the strategy and machinery of war. Suffice to say that at that critical time the leaders of either air force advanced no foolish reasons for their conflicting beliefs. From evidence accumulated during and since the war it seems that the British were right to fly at night, and that the Americans were right not to do so.

At the beginning of 1943 Churchill and Roosevelt with their military staffs met at Casablanca to plan their joint war effort. A few hours later the commander of the American Air Force in Britain, Lieutenant-General Ira C. Eaker, received the order from the Chief of Staff of the United States Army Air Forces, "Meet me in Casablanca". He was there the next morning. I quote from Morrison's book:

"Arnold was shaving when Eaker walked in. He greeted Eaker by saying, 'I've got bad news for you, son. Prime Minister Churchill has talked President Roosevelt into having the Eighth Air Force discontinue daylight bombing and join the British in the night effort."

Eaker was appalled and gave reasons.

Morrison continues:

"Arnold turned to him. 'I'll tell you what I'll do. I will make a date for you, if I can, and I think I can, to see the prime minister. I've heard him tell the president that he has a high regard for you. If you can't get him to change his mind, we're sunk.'

accumulated = made more by addition. From Latin *accumulare* ... to heap up.
adamant = unyielding; hard. From Greek *a* ... not + *daman* ... subdue; tame.
appalled = greatly shocked; dismayed. From Latin *ad* ... to + *palir* ... grow pale.
argument = chain of reasoning put forward for or against. From Latin *arguere* ... to make clear.
Casablanca = city in Morocco, North Africa.
strategy = science of planning and directing operations on a large scale in war. From Greek *strategia* ... generalship.

"The next morning Eaker went to Churchill's villa ... He waited nervously for the prime minister ... Promptly at ten o'clock, Churchill came down a stairway with the sun shining through the windows illuminating his air commodore's uniform. Eaker thought this was a good omen, knowing that Churchill usually wore the uniform of the branch of service of the man he planned to interview.

"The prime minister immediately came to the point. 'General Arnold tells me that you are unhappy about giving up daylight bombing and joining us in night bombing.'

" 'Yes, sir. In my year of service with your forces, I have heard that you always hear each side of a case before you make a decision. I've set down here, on one page, the reasons why I think it would be unfortunate for us to give up daylight bombing. All I ask is that you read this.'

"Churchill took the paper, sat down on a couch, and motioned Eaker to sit beside him."

There was then a lengthy discussion of strategy and technicalities. At last Churchill read the paper. Morrison continues:

"Eaker noticed the prime minister was reading half aloud. When he came to where Eaker had written, 'If the RAF continues at night, and the Americans by day, we shall bomb them around the clock, and they will get no rest.' He repeated 'bombing around the clock,' and reread Eaker's words, wherein he said, 'Bear in mind that by your intelligence estimates a million men are standing on the Westwall to defend against our bomber effort. These defenders – fire fighters – can be greatly reduced if we stop daylight bombing.'"

Eaker convinced Churchill. The Americans kept to day bombing.

A few days after his return to England, Eaker got an invitation from Churchill to hear his address to the House of Commons on the Casablanca Conference. Morrison tells of Eaker's growing excitement as, from his seat in the visitors' gallery he watched Churchill begin his speech.

convinced = persuaded by argument or evidence. From Latin *convincere* ... to convict of error.
Westwall = German fortifications facing England.

"It was a dramatic moment for Eaker as the now familiar voice held everyone's attention. At one point, Churchill said, 'It was there decided that our gallant RAF shall continue their effective night bombing, and the courageous Americans will continue their daylight bombing. We shall bomb the devils round the clock 'til they get no rest.' As he mentioned the words 'round the clock,' he looked at Eaker in the gallery, as if to say, 'If this is plagiarism, you must admit I acknowledge the author.' "

plagiarism = the passing off as one's own the writings or thoughts of another. It is a form of theft. From Latin *plagiarius* ... kidnapper

VIII

RUINS OF HIGH PRECISION

Vocabulary

English has such an enormous vocabulary (almost twice that of French or German) that it could shed many words without weakening itself. For example, the exact meanings of defecate, urinate and copulate are completely carried by grosser words that we all know. However, English has some high-precision words that are sole carriers of their particular meaning, and the loss of such a word's special function must weaken the language, its vocabulary not having an equally well-defined replacement for it. Alas, it is these words of special precision that are most attractive to the jackdaws of journalism, advertising, business, etc., who slightly misinterpret them from precise speakers and then botch them into approximations.

Radio and television speed these imprecisions around the world. Soon the schools are infected, children utter them, and the new collapsible pundits excuse the blurrings with, "English changes. That's usage, and usage is always right." *Claim* was an example. Here are some more:

METICULOUS = careful from fear; over-careful. From Latin *meticulosus* ... fearful; *metus* ... fear.

---

approximation = that which is near but not exactly there. From Latin *ad* ... towards + *proximus* ... near

botch = to do work clumsily

enormous = very much exceeding the usual in size or quality. One can speak of an enormous ant. From Latin *ex* ... out of + *norma* ... pattern

jackdaw = an unintelligent, talkative grabber, like the bird of that name

precision = exactness; accuracy. From Latin *prae* ... before + *caedere* ... to cut

pundit = one of great learning on a particular subject – a specialist. Like 'pedant' this term is generally not complimentary

Until it was spoilt its meaning was 'over-careful from fear'. Thus R.L. Stevenson in MEMORIES AND PORTRAITS. "Their speech, indeed, is timid; they report lions in the path; they counsel a *meticulous* footing; . . ."

'Meticulous' is used now instead of *thorough, conscientious, scrupulous, painstaking, fastidious,* or just plain *careful.*

REPLICA = an exact reproduction or copy of a work of art by the original artist. From Latin *replicare* . . . to repeat.

Now it is used instead of *facsimile, imitation, likeness, copy,* even *model.*

The BBC has been the most powerful force in the spoiling of the word. In 1979 in its popular television programme for teenagers, 'Blue Peter', the commentator, standing by a huge railway-engine, held up a model of it and said, "It's an exact replica."

DISINTERESTED = interested, but unbiased, impartial by being not privately or selfishly interested.

It took generations of usage to refine the word to that point and differentiate it clearly from 'uninterested'.

Neither 'unbiased' nor 'impartial', which are nearest to synonymity with it, can act as a general replacement for it, as each requires two or more directional bearings, whereas 'disinterested' needs only one. Accordingly, a judge before he can give an *impartial* judgment must consider at least two points of view, and if you are *unbiased* you must steer between at least two things without being pulled towards either. *'Disinterested',* however, needs only one point: Jack can have a *disinterested* interest in Jill's welfare. In that sentence 'unselfish' or 'generous' would be near synonyms for 'disinterested', but neither can be used as a general synonym for it, because each lacks the

---

facsimile = an exact copy.
model = a copy that is smaller than the original. A child may take a model of the Eiffel Tower to bed with him: he could not treat a facsimile of it so.
synonym = a word having the same or nearly the same meaning as another in the same language, e.g. *serpent, snake.*

connotation of 'impartiality' that is attached to 'disinterested': a person may be unselfish or generous yet partial or biased.

Quite apart from the unnecessary destruction of a distinction that has been used by so many fine authors, the jumbling of two such similar words as 'uninterested' and 'disinterested' on to the exact same meaning is a glaring inefficiency that should shock the commonsense of a properly taught seven year old child.

In the early 1980s I saw, with 300 million people, a BBC television broadcast of a World-Cup soccer match. Within the first two minutes of the broadcast the BBC commentator used 'disinterested' when he meant 'uninterested'.

Some correct uses:

A fair judge is *disinterested* in his cases; never uninterested.

This feeling, when *disinterested*, and connecting itself with the pure idea of duty ...

UTILITARIANISM by John Stuart Mill

"You are frank, honourable, and *disinterested*," said Mr Haredale.

BARNABY RUDGE by Charles Dickens

Her *disinterestedness*, too, has been equal to her fidelity.

QUEEN VICTORIA by Lytton Strachey

... and in short, it seemed to have been only a struggle on each side as to which should be most *disinterested* and hospitable.

PERSUASION by Jane Austen

MASSIVE is from *mass* = the quantity of matter in a body.
From Latin *massa* ... a lump.

The quintessence of 'massive' is not size, but 'a lot packed into a little space'. *Dense-heavy* is its association. A brick is more massive than a feather-pillow twice its size. A small tank crashing into the biggest bus would fold up the bus because it is more massive than the bus. Nothing could be further from

---

connotation = a meaning in addition to the main (straightforward) meaning; an association, an overtone. From Latin *com* ... together + *notare* ... to mark
quintessence = the purest, most essential part

the idea of 'hollow' or 'empty' than 'massive', yet I once heard news from the radio that an explosion "blew a *massive* hole in the side of the ship". If the news-reader had said "a square circle" or "a heavy hole" he could not have delivered purer nonsense.

Although one rightly associates 'dense' and 'heavy' with 'massive', it should be made clear in primary school that *mass* and *weight* are different concepts: weight is attached to the gravity of Earth, and as the pull of Earth's gravity varies between high mountain and low valley, an object will have more weight next to the Dead Sea than at the top of Mount Everest, and in the spaces of the Universe where there is no gravity it will have no weight at all —— but its mass is constant throughout the Universe.

Here are words that could take the weight off poor dying 'massive': big, large, tall, high, towering, fat, hulking, heavy, ponderous, great, vast, huge, enormous, immense, monstrous, elephantine, colossal, gigantic, gargantuan, tremendous, spacious, extensive, stupendous, titanic, weighty, bulky, solid, substantial, sweeping, radical.

In the election there was a *massive* swing to the Right	rather	a big swing
It was a *massive* change	rather	a sweeping or radical change
The United States has a *massive* deficit	rather	an enormous deficit
... a *massive* fire [All from the SABC]	rather	a huge fire

EXPERIENCE = knowledge resulting from observation. From Latin *experiri* ... to put to test; to try.

You cannot experience without observation. Hence an anaesthetized, unconscious patient cannot experience his operation. A road cannot experience.

Heat problems are being *experienced* with the data retrieving process of Challenger One.	rather	There are heat problems with the data retrieving process of Challenger One
Heavy thunderstorms were *experienced* in the area yesterday.	rather	There were heavy thunderstorms in the area yesterday.
Cuba has been *experiencing* a cash-flow crisis.	rather	Cuba has been in a cash-flow crisis

[All from the SABC]

Those examples are not incorrect, but they are flabby. A thinking person sees at once that the following is wrong:

X	
The roads of the Transvaal *experienced* heavy traffic.	There was heavy traffic on Transvaal roads.

[From the SABC]

LADY is to 'woman' as *gentleman* is to 'man'. In its highest sense it is applied only to a woman who is cultured, courteous, and scrupulously honest. King William IV's greatest pride was not that he was king of a great empire, but that he was considered an English gentleman.

The perfectly respectable word 'woman' is slipping out of English, and 'lady' is being spoiled in order to take its place. Nowadays almost every woman is called a lady, and this sign of mealy-mouth disease is on the tongues of reputable people. For example, in the SABC's informative weekly radio programme MEDICAL FILE, which I have listened to on-and-off over a number of years, I have heard the panel of three prominent medicos and an experienced broadcaster discuss countless women's ailments, with 'woman' and 'women' invariably mealy-mouthed to 'lady' and 'ladies'. "This is a lady's complaint ...", "Ladies should take ...". No surprise to me therefore when I recently heard a child describe a screaming, foul-mouthed drunken prostitute as "a lady" ... "and the police dragged the lady away".

Please, dear reader, help to give 'lady' back the old honour. Call a female adult a woman unless she really is a lady. To say that the Queen is a fine woman is no dishonour to her: we know she is a lady. There have, however, been kings of England who were not gentlemen, and a queen (Margaret, consort of Henry VI) who was not a lady. Shakespeare's HENRY THE SIXTH, Parts Two and Three give her unladylike character.

A child who understands the highest meanings of 'lady' and 'gentleman' is more likely in adulthood to behave well in business or on the tennis court even though he is under extreme pressure, than a person who has been brought up without respect for such distinctions.

Although extinction of prime meanings in the following examples is not so damaging as in the foregoing ones, there being other single words that can carry the prime meanings, the damage to English, and hence to all English-speaking societies, by their emasculation is still grievous because the good replacement words that must now bear the high-precision meanings are themselves weakened by deflexion from more appropriate roles, and, being not quite as well-co-ordinated for their forced roles as the maimed words were, they bring English that much closer to clumsiness.

ANTICIPATE = to foresee, and so to forestall. From Latin *anticipare* ... to take beforehand. It should not be used to mean

---

appropriate = right for the purpose; suitable. From Latin *ad* ... to + *proprius* ... one's own
deflexion = a turning away from. From Latin *de* ... from + *flectere* ... to bend
emasculation = taking away manly strength of; making feeble. From Latin *ex* ... out + *masculus* ... masculine
extinction = putting out of existence (as flames); destruction
maimed = so badly wounded as to make that part of the body useless or near useless; 'to maim' is to make crippled

"expect". It has been misused for years by the SABC. Here is a typical example: "ESCOM does not anticipate power cuts."

Of course ESCOM *did* anticipate them. It would have been incompetent of ESCOM not to do so. What the SABC meant was: ESCOM does not expect ... because it has done its best to anticipate them.

OBLIVIOUS = forgetful. It should not be used for 'unaware' or 'unconscious'. You cannot be oblivious of something unless you once knew it. From Latin *oblivisci* ... forget. 'Oblivion' is a forgetfulness.

Fowler and other masters of English have inveighed against its misuse, but to no avail. Rotten journalism, particularly over radio and television, has killed the best sense of the word. For that sense one must now use 'forgetful', 'inadvertent', or 'absent-minded'.

'Oblivious' should always take 'of'. Those who misuse it usually couple it with 'to'.

Correct Use: He stared at her now with bloodshot eyes, *oblivious of* her name that had once been so dear to him.

Misuse: Jenny forgot to tell him of the leak, so he was *oblivious to* the fact that there was no oil in the engine.

AGGRESSIVE = quick to attack without just cause. From Latin *aggredi* ... to attack. *Aggression* is an unprovoked attack. *Aggress* = to start a quarrel.

Aggression is an evil. The moral law says – Do not aggress. [From OED]

Poorly educated businessmen are the main blunters of *aggressive*. They use it instead of *enterprising, bold, active, forceful.*

ESCOM stands for Electricity Supply Commission. A huge organisation for supplying electricity in South Africa
Fowler, Henry Watson (1858–1933) Commentator on English usage and style. Famed author of A DICTIONARY OF MODERN ENGLISH USAGE

They are also gross trivializers of lofty concepts. *Strategy* and *Philosophy* are ludicrously trivialized these days by them.

STRATEGY is from Greek *strategia* ... art of the general; *strategos* ... general. It is the art and science of planning and directing military operations on the largest scale so that when a force joins battle with an enemy it is well-equipped, has efficient lines of communication, and is in the best position at the right time. That is half its stretch. The other half is so to bluff and hit the enemy before the main battle that he goes into it from an inferior position, at the wrong time, and with weakened lines of communication. Strategy then hands over an almost won battle to tactics.

Strategy is thus the highest art of war. It is the province of one who is at the very pinnacle of military command, a commander-in-chief. Names such as Napoleon and Frederick the Great spring to mind. Your life and mine have been profoundly influenced by some commanders-in-chief. For example, if Themistocles in 480 B.C. had used an inferior strategy and lost the decisive Battle of Salamis, there would probably have been no Periclean Athens, no 'glory that was Greece', and culture today from the Urals to Los Angeles would be *profoundly* different, and you and I having grown in a different culture would be profoundly different.

To use the word *strategy* for humdrum business planning is a mark of ignorance or vanity, or a combination of both. An inferior modern dictionary (LONGMAN DICTIONARY OF CONTEMPORARY ENGLISH) trivializes it thus: 'Why should he give me a present? It must be a *strategy* to make me let him go on holiday alone ... She uses *strategy* to get what she wants.'

---

c. = about. Short for Latin *circa* ... about.
concept = a general idea, e.g. Love, Charity, Courage. The idea is formed by generalization from particular examples. From Latin *con* ... together + *capere* ... to take.
lofty = very high; noble, grand; elevated in character and spirit.
profoundly = to the depths. From Latin *pro* ... for + *fundus* ... bottom.
tactics = manoeuvring in battle. From Greek *taktos* ... ordered, arranged.
Themistocles (c. 525–c.460 B.C.) Athenian statesman and general. There is an account of him in Plutarch's LIVES.
trivialize = to make little of a big thing. From Latin *trivialis* ... commonplace.
trivializer = one who trivializes.

Ruse or *ploy* for the first, and *tricks* or *cunning* or *deceit* or *plans* for the second would be better.

PHILOSOPHY, from Greek *philos* ... loving + *sophia* ... wisdom. It deals with abstract matters by logical analysis, and so suggests general principles of human conduct and morality. A wise psychologist such as William James came to it after he had mastered psychology. It is the most advanced system of thought. In his WEALTH OF NATIONS Adam Smith set out his philosophy of economics.

There are examples of prodigious musical talent flowering in childhood, but even Socrates was no philosopher as a child. Philosophy is the highest reach of human understanding and behaviour.

	rather	
An aggressive sales strategy is the *philosophy* of this company		Energetic salesmanship is the policy of this company

* * * *

Recommended for more comprehensive reading:

THE DICTIONARY OF DISEASED ENGLISH by Kenneth Hudson.
THE JARGON OF THE PROFESSIONS by Kenneth Hudson.
NEW WORDS FOR OLD by Philip Howard.
WEASEL WORDS by Philip Howard.

James, William (1842–1910) American psychologist. He wrote his great PRINCIPLES OF PSYCHOLOGY in clear, beautiful English
prodigious = so extraordinary as to inspire wonder. From Latin *prodigium* ... omen
Smith, Adam (1732–1790) The founder of modern classical economics. He was for private enterprise, and against monopoly and unwarranted state control
Socrates (c. 470–399 B.C.) Greek philospher. As Shakespeare is regarded by some as the greatest man of England, Socrates is regarded as the greatest man of classical Greece

IX

Distinctions and Avoidances of the Educated

'... when I name custom, I understand not the vulgar custom; for that were a precept no less dangerous to language than to life, if we should speak or live after the manners of the vulgar: but that I call custom of speech, which is the consent of the learned; as custom of life, which is the consent of the good.'

[DISCOVERIES by Ben Jonson]

Aim at/Aim to/Aim for

An ear for British idiom, or two seconds of commonsense will tell that *at* is better than *for* or *to*. The rifleman who aims *for* or *to* a target rather than *at* it has more hope than ability.

They aim *to* overthrow the government	rather	They aim *at* overthrowing the government
He aimed *to* be president	rather	He aimed *at* being president
He aimed *for* the heart	rather	He aimed *at* the heart

In American idiom 'aim to' is sometimes acceptable.

Beside/Besides

The first means close to, by the side of; the second, in addition to, moreover.

He sat down *beside* her and enfolded her in his arms.

"Have you any lovers *besides* me and Tom and Robert and Dick and Alan?" he inquired tenderly.

Both/Either/Each

Both and *either* refer to *two*. *Each* refers to every *one* of a group considered separately.

Both = not only one of them, but the two. Two taken together.
Either = one or the other (of two)
Each = every *one* of two or more regarded separately. ⑺₃

A football may be kicked with *either* foot

or (if you wish to show off as an acrobat) with *both* feet.

Each child had a toy (200 children, 200 toys).
You may take *either* apple (i.e. only one of the two).
You may take *both* apples (i.e. two).
Each apple costs 2 francs. Cost of two apples, 4 francs.
Both apples cost 2 francs. Cost of two apples, 2 francs.

There were cattle on *either* side of the road.	rather There were cattle on *both* sides (or *each* side) of the road.

Can/May

Can = be able to. May = have permission to.

√   X

"*May* I go to the cinema?"   "*Can* I go to the cinema?"
"No. You have not finished your homework."

If you really mean 'to be able to' then 'can' is the word. If I were unsure of my condition during convalescence from a heart attack, I might ask my doctor "Can I go to the cinema?"

Compare to/Compare with

To draws them closer together and shows that they are *alike*. *With* puts them in the balance in order to see the *difference*. Your weight can be compared *with* that of an elephant, but it cannot be compared *to* it.

√	X
to that of the world-champion.	She's the best woman player I've seen in this country. Her service and backhand can be compared *with* that of the world-champion.

Continual/Continuous

The first = very frequent; the second = uninterrupted. Think of *continual* as — — — —, and continuous as _____. *Continual* rain = rained, stopped, rained, stopped, rained, stopped. *Continuous* rain = no stop.

Criterion/Criteria

The first is singular, the second plural.

Datum/Data

The first is singular, the second plural. From Latin *datum* ... a gift, *data* ... gifts. A *datum* is a fact that is used as a basis for reasoning.

convalescence = the gradual recovery of health after illness. From Latin *com* ... completely + valescere ... to grow strong

√	X
My *data* *were* gathered from many sources.	My *data* *was* gathered from many sources.

This *datum* must be included.
[One fact]

Different from/Different to/Different than

The first is generally preferred by careful speakers and writers.

Due to/Owing to

Due to = caused by.   *Owing to* = because of.

On those distinctions Chambers 20th CENTURY
DICTIONARY is correct and admirably prescriptive, but
Webster's NEW TWENTIETH CENTURY DICTIONARY falls
badly below its generally high standard.

The terms are not interchangeable. *Owing to* can generally
replace *due to*, but not vice versa. *Due to* is therefore liable to
more mistakes. When in doubt, use *owing to*. But there should
be no doubt if the touchstones 'caused by' and 'because of' are
applied: the 'dues to' in the following three sentences are
incorrect because they cannot be replaced by *caused by*, but
they can be by *because of*.

The cat was ill *due to* bad fish.
Due to the flood the bridge was impassable.
I shall have to remain at home *due to* the serious trouble that
has overtaken me.

Owing to would be correct for those sentences.

prescriptive = authoritatively giving directions. From latin *prae* ... before + *scribere* ... to
write

The following are correct because *due to* can be replaced by
caused by

$$\checkmark$$

His inability to come was *due to* bad weather.
The accident was not *due to* carelessness.
His death, *due to* dangerous play, was a shock to all.

Each other/One another

Each other for two only, *one another* for more than two.
They killed *each other* = 2 dead. They killed *one another* = more than two dead.

Farther/Further

Use *farther* for *greater distance, further* for *in addition, besides.*
We drove *farther* down the road, and then issued a *further* statement.

Feel/Think

For sensible opinion, *thinking* is on a higher plane than *feeling*. Give more respect to 'I think that...' than to 'I feel that...'"
Football hooligans *feel* strongly and *think* weakly.

Hopefully/I hope

Leave *hopefully* for the feelers.
I hope, or *we hope*, as well as being more direct than *hopefully*, takes less time and space.

Hopefully, it will rain.   rather   I *hope* it will rain.

Less/Fewer

Fewer is for *numbers* of separate items or people. *Less* is for *quantities* that are not thought of in numbers.

There were *fewer* people in the shops because there was *less* money.

√   X

Fewer people die of ...   *Less* people die of ... (SABC's
                                    commentator in New York.)

Like/As

Most grammarians and commentators over the past hundred years have ruled against the use of *like* exampled below. Grammatical reasons will be given under GRAMMAR. Two broad differentiations are:

(i)   *Like* implies mere similarity. *As* points to complete identity.

      She is *like* a bird.
      He went to the fancy dress ball *as* a bird.
      Mrs Jones looked *like* the kidnapper, but Agnes Brown was later identified *as* the criminal. She got the baby by passing herself off *as* its mother, and it was given to her because she looked *like* its mother.

(ii) *Like* compares things, animals, people. *As* compares actions.

      She is *like* a bird.
      ('She' & 'bird' compared)
      Take a *like* amount of sugar.
      (One *amount*: another equal *amount*)
      Do [it] *as* I tell you [to do it].
      He did it *as* I do [it].
      (In both, the 'doing' actions are compared.)

To well-tuned ears the use of *like* for *as* is ugly, as in the following on the left:

Do *like* I tell you.   rather   Do *as* I tell you.
The STAR tells it like it is.   rather   The STAR tells it *as* it is.

Like I said...	rather	*As* I said...
Make *like* the world is your pudding.	rather	Take the world *as* your pudding.

A clear and lengthy article on this subject in THE RIGHT WORD AT THE RIGHT TIME (Reader's Digest), speaks against the vulgarization of *like*, but spoils the effect with this feeble recommendation: 'Except in informal contexts avoid the common mistake of using like as a straightforward conjunction ...' I say avoid it *especially* in informal contexts: children, politicians or businessmen may be listening.

THE ELEMENTS OF STYLE by Strunk and White deals admirably with the matter of *like* & *as*.

Like/Love

Write to us; we'd *love* to hear from you. (BBC WORLD SERVICE)	rather	Write to us; we'd *like* (or very much *like*) to hear from you.

Phenomenon/Phenomena

The first is singular, the second plural.

One/You/Him/He/Himself, etc.

Do not change in midstream. Keep to the one you begin with.

What can *one* do when *one* finds *oneself* drowning?	What can *one* do when *he* finds *himself* drowning?
One cannot have it both ways, can *one*?	*One* cannot have it both ways, can *you*?
What can *you* do when *you* find *yourself* drowning?	
You cannot have it both ways, can *you*?	

Prepared to/Willing to

Prepare is from Latin *praepare* ... to make ready. That is the meaning it has in English. Thus 'I am *prepared* to go on holiday' does not mean 'I am willing to go on holiday' but implies 'My bags are packed, and I'm ready to leave'. If your answer is 'No', give it directly.

I am not *prepared* to grant your request.

rather

I *will* not grant your request.

or

I *shall* not grant your request. (A stronger No)

Shall/Will
Should/Would

Properly applied, they bring greater subtlety and precision to English. More will be said of them under GRAMMAR. Here ⑨⑧ read the samples again and again so that your ear and eye become trained to the main senses of the words, and their idiomatic drifts. Once you have grasped their sense and sound you will rise above their less efficient use, which is almost universal, and apply them with easy competence. Some of the examples are old-fashioned. For instance

I would come if you *should* ask me
   would now usually be
I would come if you asked me
              or
I'd come if you asked me.

Nevertheless, train your ear to the older forms so as to be naturally in tune when you come across them in the older classics.

One of the main senses: when you put *yourself* into the future, *shall* and *should* express plain likelihood or certainty, and *will* and *would* express determination (will-power), command, desire or promise.

drifts = meanings

67

Likelihood or Certainty	Determination, Command, Wish
I *shall* do it.	I *will* do it. [Determination, Desire or Promise]
I *shall* die some day.	I *will* die tomorrow, either by taking poison or by shooting myself. [Determination]
I *shall* go to school tomorrow. I have no choice.	I *will* go to school tomorrow, even though I'm ill. [Determination]
Next month I *shall* ask you to help him.	I *will* help him. [Promise]
I *shall* be glad to see you. [The gladness is certain. He is a friend]	I *will* do my best to pay my debts. [Promise]
I *shall* never succeed.	I *will* never succeed. I don't like myself.

Likelihood or Certainty	Determination, Command, Wish
"We *shall* fight on the beaches, we *shall* fight on the landing grounds, we *shall* fight in the fields and in the streets, we *shall* fight in the hills; we *shall* never surrender." [Winston Churchill, 1940]	

That passage has been criticised for having *shalls* instead of *wills*, but I think Churchill was quite right. The determination was taken for granted. He was stating certainty.

For Yourself

Likelihood or Certainty	Determination, Command, Wish
I *shall* not do it.	I *will* not do it.
[Certainty]	[Determination]
Usually said:	Usually said:
I *shan't* do it.	I *won't* do it.
I *shall* be delighted to come on Friday.	
I expect we *shall* come.	
I *shall* not invoke the aid of the police against him.	

When *you* ask a question, you give the person the *shall* or *will* that you expect him to give in his answer:

"*Shall* you be in Johannesburg tomorrow?"	"*Will* you be going to Johannesburg tomorrow?" (= Is it your intention to go?)
"I *shall*."	"I *will*."
Shall I send it?	"*Will* you take this woman?"
	"I *will*."
What *shall* we do with the drunken sailor? (You are asking for a command)	

Shall and *will* look to the future from the present (now). *Should* and *would* show how you viewed the future once upon a time.

I asked whether I *should* send it.	I know I said I *would* not do it, but as soon as he kissed me all my determination left me, and I did it.
He said I *should* be ill if I drank that.	

For Yourself

Likelihood or Certainty	Determination, Command, Wish
I said I *should* die some day.	I knew I *would* do it.

For Yourself

Likelihood or Certainty

He knew well that I *should* never willingly invoke the aid of the police against him. [A. Conan Doyle]

When you put *others* (who are not attached to you by 'we') into the future, *will* and *would* express plain likelihood or certainty, and *shall* and *should* express determination (will-power), command, desire or promise. In other words — the general rule that applies to *yourself* in the future is exactly reversed for *others* in the future.

For Others

Likelihood or Certainty	Determination, Command, Wish
He *will* do it.	He *shall* do it. It is commanded.
All *will* die some day. There is a fear that he *will* skip bail.	You *shall* be taken hence to a place of execution, and hanged by the neck until you are dead. [Judge's command]
They *will* not be rewarded.	You shall be rewarded. [Promise]
Thieves *will* steal.	Thou shalt not steal. [Command]
He *will* never succeed. He is too much of a fool.	He *shall* never succeed. I have planned his downfall.
He *will* not regret his generosity. He is not changeable.	You *shall* give the drunken sailor no more drink. [Command]
"Courage *will* come and go." [Sheridan]	So long as a Spartan stands, no enemy *shall* pass. [Determination]

As with 'For Yourself', *should* and *would* show how the future was viewed once upon a time, but when they are applied to

70

others they generally conform to the reversed roles of *shall* and *will* as above.

For Others

Likelihood or Certainty	Determination, Command, Wish
He said he *would* do it.	It was recommended that he *should* do it.
It was clear that he *would* never succeed. He was too much of a fool.	I said that you *should* be rewarded. Here is your reward.

Those are clear-cut usages of *shall, will, should* and *would*. Their following idiomatic applications do not conform to such easy rules. Therefore, even more than with the foregoing examples — absorb their sense by sounding them again and again.

I *should* like to have your friendship.
I *would* have your friendship. *Would* there and in the next two examples = *should like*, but its sense of desire is stronger.

> Break, break, break,
> On thy cold grey stones, O Sea!
> And I *would* that my tongue could utter
> The thoughts that arise in me. [Tennyson]

Would that I were there.

I *should* like to be there. Note that *should* carries no sense of desire. The desire in *should like* is carried by *like*. If *would* (when *you* use it) = *should like*, logic and good English agree that *I would like* is not the best English. But note that (when *you* do not put yourself in) such statements as *He would like to go* are perfectly correct.

I am anxious that a gentleman *should* be selected as captain.

I *shall* be delighted to see you. I *should* be delighted to see you. In the first statement there is no doubt about his coming. In the second there is doubt.

Tennyson, Alfred Lord (1809–1892) One of the greatest English poets. The only British poet to be given a peerage

71

I am at a loss as to what *I should* do. [Doubt]

If he *should* come, I *should* go. [The first *should* expresses doubt as to his coming. The second *should* carries certainty as to my going]

How *should* I know? How *would* you know?

As I boarded the bus, whom *should* I see but my wife arm in arm with a man I did not know. [Here *should* = fated to]

I know that I *should* do it, but I feel so lazy this morning. [*Should* here in the present time (now), and = ought to]

The rains *should* stop [*should* here = are likely to] today.

Should you like tea or coffee in the morning? (I *should* like to have tea, please)

Should you like to come with me? (Yes, I *should*)

In both the questions, *should* expresses doubt. In the following it expresses the doubt of a contingency.

> If I *should* die, think only this of me:
> That there's some corner of a foreign field
> That is for ever England . . .
>
> [THE SOLDIER by Rupert Brooke)

This plucking at his left ear was his most flagrant habit: he *would* do it even on the stage, and it was his last act before he died. [Here *would* = used to]

He *will* pluck at his left ear. He even does it on the stage. [Here *will* = keeps on doing]

Should and *would* soften the tone of command that is carried in *shall*, and sometimes in *will*. "You *will* go to your room!" is given and taken as a most peremptory command. Why then does it have *will* instead of *shall*? ("You *shall* go to your room" is also a strong command, but not so strong as the former). The logic of the apparent illogicality is similar to that of the Churchill example: the speaker takes it as a certainty that the one

Brooke, Rupert (1887–1915) Died on active service in the First World War. He is buried on Skyros, a Greek island in the Aegean

contingency = something liable but not certain to happen. Its happening depends on something else. From Latin *contingere* . . . in contact

peremptory = that admits no refusal. From Latin *peremptorius* . . . decisive; deadly

addressed will go to his room. "*Would* you go to your room and tidy it, please" is a softer command. "Managers of soccer clubs *should* submit their returns to this department before the 31st December." There *should* rather than *shall* makes the injunction less peremptory.

Someone, Somebody, Nobody, Everybody, Everything, Anything, Anyone, Each, Every

They should never be thought of as plural.

You saw earlier that *each* refers to every *one* of a group. The rest also point at *one*. Commonsense tells that *-body* of *somebody*, *everybody*, *nobody* and *anybody* cannot be plural. The same with the endings *-thing* and *-one*. All those endings proclaim singularity.

There are instances of eminent authors coupling those words illogically with plurals, but such exalted lapses are in a very small minority. Therefore, follow the first-class majority, the most respected grammarians, and your own commonsense. Make all words singular that are related to them in a statement.

Each soldier fired *his* rifle.	rather than	*Each* soldier fired *their* rifles.
Everybody who fired *was* a crack shot.	rather than	*Everybody* who fired *were* crack shots.
Every sergeant, corporal and private *was* a crack shot.	rather than	*Every* sergeant, corporal and private *were* crack shots.
Anyone is liable to make a mistake in *his* income tax return. [Note that in such a context *his* stands for female as well as male]	rather than	Anyone is liable to make a mistake in *their* income tax return.
Someone is going to fire *his* rifle.	rather than	Someone is going to fire *their* rifle.

73

Note the general difference between *each* and *every*. *Each* separates individuals one at a time from the group, and does not consider the group. *Every* gathers together the individuals one at a time, and relates them to the group. They both mean *all*, but one at a time. They can be figured thus:

EACH

EVERY

Each went his own separate way.

Every person in the group worked towards the common good.

Note another difference between them. The group upon which *each* is applied may comprise as few as two individuals. *Every*'s group must have more than two individuals.

Student/Pupil

The first is engaged in study at a university or other place of higher education. The second is applied to schoolchildren. The person who calls schoolchildren 'students' is most likely to commit the other gaffes exemplified in this chapter.

primary school pupils
high school pupils

Primary school students
high school students

Stratum/Strata

The first is singular, the second plural.

Unrest/Violence

To delineate the difference would be to undervalue your intelligence. I trust that a description of a bloody riot as an 'unrest situation' will be marked by you as idiotic.

gaffes = blunders

Were/Was

When you want to express doubt, wish or an imaginary condition, use *were*. Otherwise use *was*.

Were	*Was*
I wish I *were* a rich man.	When I *was* a rich man.
If I *were* you ...	I was so mad I thought I *was* you. [This really happened]
She treated me as if I *were* a baby.	In her madness she really thought I *was* a baby.
If she *were* screaming now you would hear her.	If she *was* screaming there, you must have heard her. [Fact]

X

I wish I *was* you

Who/Whom

With *who* and *whom* too many English-speaking adults are defeated by a simple rule of grammar that in German does not unbalance a small German child. Over the past five centuries indeed some of the best English authors have tripped over them. But, as in the case of *each* & *every* group, gross mistakes among these authors were atypical, and I believe that each erring author would immediately have corrected his blunder had it been pointed out to him.

Surely the best remedy is not, as some have suggested, to do away with *whom* altogether (and so to lower the standard to that of the incompetent), but to ground primary school children in a simple rule of grammar that will make them secure not only with *who* and *whom,* but also with other logical distinctions, such as those between *I* and *me,* and *she* and *her,* etc. How strange and stuffy will English literature from Shakespeare to Bertrand Russell with all its *whoms* appear to a future

atypical = not representative of the group. From Greek *a* ... not + *tupos* ... type generation that, having lost all ability to discriminate between even *I* and *me*, has sunk to "Me want cohabit Jane" usage. Have no doubt that by then the consensus of "progressive educational" authority in the pidgin linguistics will be "English doesn't need such outmoded stuff. Give it up".

The grammar upon which *who* and *whom* are founded will be given in GRAMMAR. The following examples are for sight and sound.

04 (105)

Who	**Whom**
Who are you?	*Whom* shall I marry?
Who do you think you are?	It does not matter *whom* you marry.
Who was he?	*Whom* should I ask?
Who did you say he was?	*Whom* is this for?
This is the person *who* wrote the letter.	For *whom* is this?
This is the person *who* I believe wrote the letter.	*Whom* are you writing to? To *whom* are you writing?
Who is your barrister for the case?	I don't know *whom* to get.
Who he is is not important.	*Whom* are you representing?
It was she *who* would be hurt.	*Whom* did you tell?
It was she *who* I saw would be hurt.	
My eldest son, Robert, *who* is very clever, I entered for university.	My eldest son, Robert, *whom* I entered for university, is very clever.
Who are the expert thieves?	These are the thieves *whom* it is impossible to detect.

Who	Whom
He gave the money to whoever asked. [Whoever = the one who]	Give the money to *whomever* you wish. [Whomever = the one whom]
	"Any man's death diminishes me, because I am involved in Mankind. And therefore never send to know for *whom* the bell tolls. It tolls for thee." DEVOTIONS (1624) by John Donne

* * * * * * * *

INDEX TO A BROADCASTING STATE OF MIND

The following exchange of letters was occasioned by the BBC's faulty grammar in its advice to foreigners desirous of improving their English. The advice came from one of its BBC ENGLISH magazines as follows:

Here are some important points to remember when you write a postcard (or letter for that matter):

- **WHO** Who are you writing to?
- **WHY** What is the reason for sending the card?
- **WHAT** What do you want to say in the card?
- **WHERE** Where are you? Where is the person you are sending the card to?
- **HOW** How will you express your message?

Let's see how this plan works in the usual situation when we write postcards, which is when we are on holiday.

Dear Jim,
Having a lovely time on a sailing barge. Wish you were here too. Beautiful weather, no rain. Easy journey, flight half empty. Boat is very comfortable and food on board er... interesting. We cook it ourselves! People very friendly, even when we collide with their boats.
Love,
Tracy

J. Johnson Esq.,
19 Pandora Road,
Piltdown,
Sussex.

Johannesburg.
20/9/1983

To Miss Sue Cokyll,
c/o BBC English,
P.O. Box 76,
Bush House,
London WC2 B4PH,
England.

Dear Madam,

I hope that the cutting herewith of my article* will be useful.
Yours faithfully,
Ian Bruton-Simmonds

* Part of the article:

"This mistake of *who* for *whom* is in the latest issue of that most influential magazine BBC ENGLISH (page 20), which is published by the British Broadcasting Corporation for foreign students of English. In a two-page spread on how to write a postcard Miss Sue Cokyll 'Who are you writing to?' I shall send her a copy of this article!"

British Broadcasting Corporation,
London.
8th November, 1983

Dear Mr Bruton-Simmonds,

The cutting from the newspaper 'Sowetan' which you sent to Ms. Cokyll has been forwarded to me.

The articles in BBC ENGLISH to which you refer was written in the colloquial style. Hence the expression, "*Who are you writing to?*"

However, normally I would agree with you that this kind of construction should be avoided.

I was pleased to read your comment about BBC ENGLISH being 'that most influential magazine', **(sic)** I hope it continues to be so!

Yours sincerely,

Hilary Ferguson
Editorial Assistant,
English by Radio and Television

Johannesburg.
2/12/1983

Dear Miss Ferguson,

Your letter of 8th November defends the indefensible: there was no explanation or warning to those who need it that the construction was 'colloquial'; indeed, the sentence Miss Cokyll had was not colloquial at all, but a serious question to her readers.

The SOWETAN newspaper (cuttings herewith) is at present in the middle of a serial essay of mine on points of English that readers of your magazine are certainly in need of. If you would like to see the essay I should gladly send you a copy for you to consider publishing in your magazine.

Yours sincerely,
Ian Bruton-Simmonds.

There was no reply to that letter.

As regards postcards in English, will my readers please note that

(i) Although there is nothing wrong in writing, as in a letter, "Dear Jim" and "Love", it is customary to omit greetings,

---

item = a detail of information. Latin *item* ... just so

obliterate = rub out. From Latin *obliterare* ... to strike out

(sic) = thus so. Draws attention to a mistake in what is being quoted. The comma was a mistake. It should have been a full stop. Latin *sic* ... so, thus

endings and date on account of a postcard's little space. The date (correctly omitted in the example) will be given by the postmark cancellation of the postage stamp. The magazine ought to have mentioned those two items.

(ii) The address in the example is too high up: the postmark over the postage stamp would probably obliterate part of it.

You may wonder at my mentioning, in such a short book on English, a practical post office procedure that has nothing to do with language; but attention to that example is valid. One cannot fail, if one looks about with perceptive eyes, to notice every day that careless language and unpracticality go together. Indeed, that is perhaps the most important point made in this book.

The following letter is (I hope) representative of the fundamental quality of the BBC. It answers in straightforward fashion my criticism of a classical author's context horribly wrenched to "colloquial style".

BBC BROADCASTING HOUSE
LONDON W1A 1AA

12 September 1980

Dear Mr Simmonds,

Thank you for your letter of the 1st September concerning the unlikely use of the expression "like you used to do" in an ancient adaptation of the Barchester Chronicles, by Constance Cox.

I totally agree with you. Trollope would have never used words like that in the mouth of an intelligent person – a low class person maybe!

I can only hope that any producer or actor, at the time of production, would pick up such inappropriate usage and I hope such misexpression would not go out on the air. If it did, post hoc, I apologise.

Yours sincerely

(John Tydeman)
Assistant Head of Drama, Radio.

post hoc = after this (Pure Latin)

X

A Warning Against a Modern Trend of English

You should know by now that there has been a steep decline in the quality of everyday English, and you no doubt wonder why and how the decline has come about. Indeed, if you are English-speaking, it is vital for your success and the success of your children that you do have a clear understanding of what has been a disaster in education throughout the English-speaking world. Only from such understanding can catastrophe be prevented and improvement begin.

The most revealing thing about a man or a society is language. "A man's character appears more by his words than, as some think it does, by his looks" says Plutarch, a celebrated historian. "As the language is, so is the nation" says Jespersen, an authority on English grammar.

Language is supremely important because in dealing with people a man gives and receives most thoughts in words. Language, being his main connection with humanity, is by far his most valuable possession; but it is not his private possession. He has this verbal wealth in common with his fellow men. If the language is improved by a great writer, he and his fellows are richer; if it is deteriorated by a greatly influential broadcaster he and his whole society are poorer — poorer because their most important undertaking, communication, is being done with a less efficient tool, and if the spoilings are numerous and widespread, inevitably some of that society's important *actions* will become less efficient.

The main efficients of language, as of action, are Accuracy

---

catastrophe = a sudden and final disaster. From Greek *katastophe* ... an overthrowing
Jespersen, Otto (1860 – 1943) A Dane. One of the foremost authorities on the English language

and Brevity. They, when perfectly harnessed together, carry the complete thought or action in the shortest time.

In disordering higher education and in killing millions of the first-rate youth of two successive generations, the two World Wars made critical gaps in leadership all over the Western world, and for want of the best the gaps had to be filled in many cases with inferior people. These inferiors have weakened Western society everywhere, but most harmfully in the schools and universities, where as teachers they have blunted language just at a period when quick and fine accuracy in comprehension and expression was most needed to deal with the tremendous flood of scientific and technical information that is upon us and changing the world.

The harm done by them stems from their weakness in the Humanities, in which they are either insensitive or (the majority of them) almost completely ignorant.

The Humanities have been predominant in forming Western character, feeling and languages. They are carried mainly in language, and their bases are respect for the individual, and respect for facts.

Respect for the individual affirms friendship, individual freedom and initiative, and abhorrence of intellectua servility. Two statements on that basis:

"... if I had to choose between betraying my country and betraying my friend, I hope I should have the guts to betray my country." E.M. Forster.

"I disapprove of what you say, but I will defend to the death your right to say it." Voltaire.

Respect for facts affirms Reason from Facts, and hence, practical accuracy and devotion to Truth. The ideal is exemplified in Ben Jonson's:

"... without truth all the actions of mankind are craft, malice,

Forster, Edward Morgan (1879 - 1970) English novelist. Believed that sensitivity in personal relations was the most important thing. His best known novels are HOWARD'S END, A PASSAGE TO INDIA, and A ROOM WITH A VIEW.

Voltaire (1694 - 1778) Philosopher, playwright, historian. Through his devastating wit and passion he influenced Western thought and action. He believed in the dignity of the individual, free inquiry, and freedom of conscience. Was greatly influenced by John Locke.

or what you will, rather than wisdom ... I will have no man addict himself to me; but if I have anything right, defend it as Truth's, not mine ... It profits not me to have any man fence or fight for me ... Stand for Truth, and 'tis enough."

The Humanities pervade the best European literature, especially its poetry and history. As all the various Western nations have a common cultural foundation in the literatures of the ancient Greeks, Romans and Jews, a man badly deficient in understanding of Greco-Roman and Judaic-Christian history and literature is an outcast in his own national culture, for the national literary giants (Dante, Italy – Rabelais, France – Cervantes, Spain – Shakespeare, England – Goethe, Germany) all wrote in a Christian society that was imbued with religion from the Bible, and they studded their writings with reference and allusion to Greco-Roman myth, history and philosophy, taking it for granted that their readers knew those grounds.

A Western man out of tune with the best literature of his own nation is adrift from the prime wisdom of his forefathers. He is therefore uneducated, and hardly fit to teach rudiments. His ignorance will show in his language. In higher teaching, untuned, longwinded, inaccurate, his language will ill-form, muddle or stifle his ideas, and make him a misleader, not a teacher. Even in mathematics and science (which seem far from poetry and history), though he is highly intelligent and has good degrees, his understanding and teaching of those subjects, whenever he attempts high flights, will be weighed down by poor imagination: intellectually he can never be in the class of

ch. = chapter

Cervantes, Miguel de (1547 – 1616) Spanish novelist who gave us DON QUIXOTE. "There are but two families in the world, as my grandmother used to say, the Haves and the Have-nots." DON QUIXOTE ch. 20

Dante, Alighieri (1263 – 1321) Greatest Italian poet. In his greatest work, THE DIVINE COMEDY, he shows that Virgil, the greatest Roman poet, is his guide. "There is no greater sorrow than to recall a time of happiness in misery". DIVINE COMEDY

Goethe, J.W. von (1749 – 1832) Improved the German language in his vast output of poetry and prose. "Man errs, 'till his strife is over." FAUST

Rabelais, Francois (c. 1494 – c. 1533) French. His great work GARGANTUA AND PANTA-GRUEL derides false learning

rudiments = first steps. From Latin *rudimentum* ... a rude (simple) thing

Shakespeare (1564 – 1616) You know who he is

stifle = to stop air getting in so that it can't breathe

the great scientists and mathematicians of the Western World, who, as shown by the elegance of their language, were all in tune with their national literature.

In the general decline of Western culture, English has suffered most grievously. In the English-speaking countries, a language inefficient and out of tune with all good written or spoken English, a language that would have marked a man out as uneducated three generations ago, is now the vogue in many influential circles: the *majority* of psychiatrists, psychologists, sociologists (who all deal with *human* problems!) use it, and, English being now the predominant international language, this debasement of it is spread the world over by scientific and technical journals and international symposia — to the detriment of millions of foreigners who copy it.

Two great strengths of English, simplicity and richness, stultify the poorly educated who go beyond their ability.

"Oh how easy" sums up the early impression of many foreign students of English, and they are right. Grammatically, English is simple, free from the rigid rules requiring Germans, Frenchmen, Spaniards and Russians to step carefully in their sentences; and its key words —— little verbs, and prepositions that can also act as adverbs —— in combination have marvellous power to fit almost any context. Its grammar and idiom, like the British Constitution, are established more by precedent and example than by formality and injunction.

Indeed, at home before the First World War, injunctions were hardly needed, for all educated Englishmen had laboured and been disciplined in at least one foreign field of grammar, Latin; and feeling for the natural rhythms, idioms and grammar of their own language had been instilled into them since early childhood by good conversation of elders imbued with good English literature; and those among the less well-educated classes of Englishmen who wished to rise in the world improved their language by copying that of the educated class —

injunction = an authoritative command. From Latin *in* ... + *jungere* ... to join (to join the command with authority)
instilled = poured slowly drop by drop. From Latin *in* ... in + *stilla* ... a drop
stultify = to make a person look foolish. From Latin *stultus* ... *foolish* + *facere* ... to make
vogue = fashion of the time

and even the uneducated, since 1611 when the Authorised Version of the Bible was heard regularly in churches over the length and breadth of England, had the sound of superb English as a touchstone for their speech and understanding.

But that was before the World Wars and electronic broadcasting. Nowadays, electronically, a relatively few brazen illiterates are magnified and proliferated monstrous models to millions who have neither the education nor the ear to withstand a perpetual battery of bad taste; and proper leaders who would easily have ridiculed such vulgarians from the gates of influence are dead or too few.

I take it for granted that an intelligent person intending to learn English seriously does not wish to load himself with an inferior English just to be one with the huge class of English-speakers who are stuck with it through bad schooling and lack of good reading in their homes. Your good taste makes you eager to know and to use good English, and from the beginning your path to that goal should be clear.

If you would reach the goal BEWARE OF THE ENGLISH VOCABULARY. It is a deep quagmire to foreigners and badly educated English-speakers alike. Its danger lies in its combination of simplicity and richness.

The simplicity and the richness derive from two distinct sources. English is really a mixture of two languages. Its vocabulary was brought down by two mighty, equal-sized rivers, the Germanic and the Latinate. From the Germanic come words that every person born to English is at home with: HEAVEN, HELL, LOVE, HATE, DEATH, FATHER, MOTHER, WATER, OX, DOG, WORD he never needs to look up in a dictionary —

Authorised Version: By order of King James I the Bible was put into the best English by the most learned men of Shakespeare's time. Called the 'King James Version', it is the most successful translation ever made, and the greatest literary work in the English language. It was revised about 100 years ago by a committee of British and American scholars and called the 'Revised King James Version'

brazen = like brass, harsh, loud, insensitive, shameless

derive = flows from; grows from. From Latin *de* ... from + *rivus* ... a stream

distinct = clearly not alike. From Latin *dis* ... apart + *stinguere* ... to prick; to pierce (to mark)

proliferated = rapidly multiplied. From Latin *proles* ... offspring + *ferre* ... to bear

touchstone = a stone for testing the purity of gold or silver, hence a test of quality; a standard of judgement

nor the words in the following two lists of Germanic words. These few Germanic words that are the main verbs, prepositions, adverbs and conjunctions are the core of the English language.

Verbs	Prepositions, adverbs, conjunctions	
BE	about	adv. & prep.
CAN	across	adv. & prep.
COME	against	prep.
DO	after	prep. adv. & conj.
GET	along	adv.
GIVE	and	conj.
GO	as	prep. adv. & conj.
HAVE	at	prep.
KEEP	away	prep. & adv.
LET	back	adv.
MAKE	because	conj.
MAY	before	prep. & conj.
PUT	between	prep. & adv.
SAY	beyond	prep. & adv.
SEE	but	prep, adv. & conj.
SEEM	by	prep. & adv.
SEND	down	prep. & adv.
SHALL	for	prep. & conj.
TAKE	from	prep.
WILL	how	adv.
	if	conj.
	in	prep. & adv.
	inside	prep. & adv.
	near	prep.
	of	prep.
	off	prep. & adv.
	on	prep. & adv.
	or	conj.
	out	adv.
	over	prep. & adv.
	round (around)	prep. & adv.
	since	prep. adv. & conj.
	than	prep. & conj.
	there	adv.
	through	adv.
	to	prep.
	together	adv.

Prepositions, adverbs, conjunctions

under	prep. & adv.
unless	conj.
up	prep. & adv.
when	adv. & conj.
where	adv. & conj.
with	prep.

Those twenty verbs when combined with fitting Germanic prepositions or adverbs have kaleidoscopic ability to express a huge variety of thoughts. For example, see from the diagram how the verb GIVE, supported by eight words from the second list, can, like a versatile ballet dancer, hold many different positions gracefully; and that it can always connect with the Latinate zone of the language, the words of which, as you can see from a good dictionary, are generally described through Germanic verb and preposition, or Germanic verb and adverb.

You will see from the diagram that the Latinate part of English is made up of longer words. Generally these words are not supple or homely like the Germanic ones, but grave and exact. They bring in fine shades of meaning with stately sound and rhythm.

It is the apt balance of Germanic and Latinate by good speakers and writers over hundreds of years that has made English vigorous, exact and flexible. Here are three sentences through the GIVE DOWN channel of the diagram:

1. The pompous ass GIVES DOWN (PONTIFICATES) his opinion each time as if it were the Cullinan diamond.

---

diagram = an outline drawing for making something more easily understandable. From Greek *dia* ... across + *graphein* ... to write

kaleidoscope in Greek means 'beautiful shapes to be seen'. A kaleidoscope is a tube whose end contains two mirrors and small pieces of coloured glass. If one looks into the tube and rotates it, the mirrors reflect the coloured glass in constantly changing symmetrical patterns

pompous = full of self-importance. From Latin *pompa* ... a solemn procession

pontificate = speaking with the pomp and dignity of a pope (usually ridiculously). From Latin *pontifex* ... Roman high priest

versatile = turning easily; many-sided in talent. From Latin *versare* ... turning easily and frequently

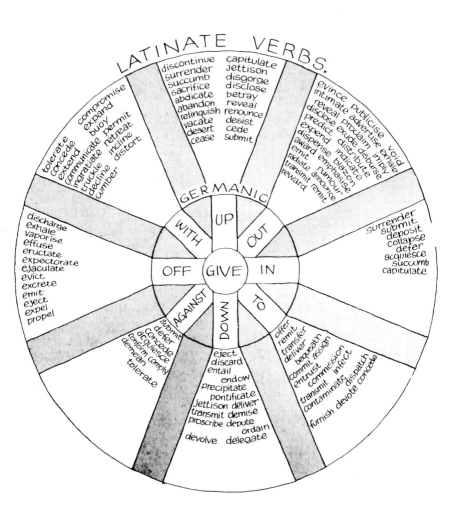

2. The King is pleased to GIVE DOWN (DEPUTE) to you his authority over the province.
3. 0 Poseidon, to save ourselves from the fury of the sea we miserable sailors GIVE DOWN (JETTISON) both cargo and private possessions to your deep.

The two surest signs of a badly educated English-speaking person are:

(i) <u>Improper connection between Germanic and Latinate sense.</u> A great deal of Latinate sense is foreign to him, but instead of using a short Germanic or an easy word from the Latinate that he understands, he will, through desire to sound learned, mis-apply a long Latinate. For instance, he will mean WAS NEEDY or POOR [little money] IN CHILDHOOD, but will say WAS DISADVANTAGED [unfavourable conditions] in CHILD-HOOD. Wouldn't you agree that an only child whose multi-millionaire father is a drunken bully and mother a homicidal maniac who tries frequently to hurl him overboard from the family yacht or drown him in the mansion's heated swimming-pool is more disadvantaged than a child in a poor but loving family?

(ii) <u>Lack of feeling for rhythm, euphony and idiom.</u> For ex-ample in the following sentence his ear would not register the knock-kneed rhythm, the cacophonous iteration of TION and ITY, and the faulty idiom of AIM FOR.

In the articulatory transmis<u>sion</u> of informa<u>tion</u> in an educa<u>tion</u> situa<u>tion</u> the func<u>tion</u> of an effective teacher-communica<u>tion</u> which

---

articulate = speak. (See next entry)
articulatory = to do with fitting one joint into another. In this context, the joining of sounds to make speech
cacophonous = ugly sounding. (Opposite to 'euphonious') From Greek *kakos* ... bad + *phone* ... voice
depute = to appoint as one's substitute. From Latin *deputare* ... to give your right to somebody so that he has your authority
iteration = something uttered repeatedly. From Latin *iterum* ... again
jettison = to throw overboard to lighten a ship or aircraft in time of danger. From Latin *jactare*... to throw hard

aims for broad culture-value simila<u>rity</u> and not exclusi<u>vity</u> and multiform<u>ity</u> may be impeded by out-dated elitist concep<u>tions</u>.

Translated into respectable English those silly ideas might run

> *Teachers wishing to stress cultural similarity and banish all signs of social class-distinction from their teaching may unwittingly impede their wish by allowing out-of-date upper-class ideas to obtrude when speaking to their pupils.*

It is such abominations whose foul phrase and inexact thought make the orthodox language of modern commerce and industry and the social sciences so contrary to the common genius of English and Science.

What is the basis of that genius? ACCURATE BREVITY. In English even euphony has been sacrificed to brevity in a process that for centuries has been dropping euphonious vowels from words, and words from sentences. Examples:

In 1350 NAME was pronounced with both vowels; by 1550 its "e" was mute. In 1550 the "ion" suffix in words such as DECIS-ION that is now sounded "in" was then still pronounced with both vowels; and the "e" in past tenses such as PASSED was still clearly sounded (as in "sounded", but more deliberately); and there was still an "eth" termination as in WALKETH, which was pronounced with the "e" and the "th", both of which are now replaced by a single harsh "s" (WALKS), which is not euphonious as was the longer, softer "eth", but is much quicker. Words have also been shortened by cutting off whole sections: omnibus/BUS, cabriolet/CAB, petroleum/PETROL, pianoforte/PIANO, withdrawing-room/DRAWINGROOM, and "influenza" and "telephone" will soon be formally written as "flu" and "phone". Sentences have been compressed, sometimes in the face of disapproving grammarians, without loss of meaning. HE DRESSED HIMSELF became HE DRESSED.

---

euphonious = pleasant sounding. (Opposite to 'cacophonous') From Greek *eu* ... well + *phone* ... voice.
orthodox = currently thought right. From Greek *orthos* ... straight (correct) + *doxa* ... opinion.

"Which" is commonly left out of THAT IS THE HOUSE which I HAVE BOUGHT. See what Shakespeare leaves out of the two following sentences (what is left out is in small): NO EVIL that is LOST IS WAIL'D for WHEN IT IS GONE. THE THIEF DOTH FEAR EACH BUSH to be AN OFFICER.

My argument comes now to the main reason why so many English-speaking people commonly regarded as well-educated on account of university degree or high position are really ill-educated: they have not learnt respect for brevity or accuracy because they have not read even one great English classic properly, and what they read and write is only by sight, never by sound. Hence the paradox that almost any Cockney bus conductor or English farm-labourer with not much Latinate English but with customary straightforwardness and fine collo-quial ear speaks far better English and has incomparably keener understanding of anything he cares to put his mind to than the stock English-speaking sociology graduate, who has a jumble of jargon Latinate and some ostentatious mathematics quite unfitted to his vague intellect: the working-men think and *hear* in clear English, the other flounders in a quagmire.

May the time soon come when real scholarship, science, and English-speaking common-sense look critically at the simulacra

---

Cockney = a working-class Londoner who speaks in a typical London dialect
colloquial = to do with common everyday informal talk. From Latin *com* ... together + *loqui* ... to speak
flounders = makes violent, awkward movements that do not achieve much
jargon = the technical language of a science, profession, craft, trade or sport ———

silly mid-on	in	cricket
oolong	in	the tea trade
tatting	in	lace-making
apophyge	in	architecture
meson	in	nuclear physics ———

all are perfectly good jargon for specialists. However, when a fool uses a specialized word such as 'methodology' in the wrong context for no other reason than to pretend that he's a scientist or a philosopher, *his* jargon = language artificial and uneducated, used for showing-off
ostentatious = boastful, showing-off. From Latin *ostentus* ... showing; display
paradox = something apparently absurd but really true. From Greek *para* ... beyond + *doxa* ... opinion
simulacra = deceptive substitutes as unlike the real things as their shadows. From Latin *simulare* ... to make a false show of; to feign
stock = average; ordinary; run-of-the-mill

of education who are now dignified only because few sensible people have taken the trouble to look carefully at their ridiculous pretensions.

The simple truth is that today the social sciences, especially sociology, have been vitiated by the very lowest pedantry (pedantry that stuffs itself with inane writings), and are growing dumps not only of ill-education but also of *innate unintelligence*: no young person with even a glimmer of common-sense would give three years of his study to the stodge called sociology that is offered at most English-speaking universities around the world. I have known intelligent undergraduates who mistakenly wandered into sociology, but each left it in disgust (and amusement) after easily passing the first year examination.

Those of you who have English as a second language — if you have good taste in your language — you should, with some attention to the pointers already given, soon acquire ability to distinguish between firm and flabby English, even though you may never rise to fluency in speaking and writing English. Such discrimination will give you tremendous advantage in important dealings with English-speaking people, for from Ben Jonson's dictum "Language most shows a man: Speak, that I may see thee" you can deduce the golden rule: HE THAT SPEAKS OR WRITES INEFFICIENTLY WILL ACT INEFFICIENTLY.

---

deduce = by reasoning to go from a general fact (or supposed general fact) to a particular one. From Latin *de* ... from + *ducere* ... to lead
dictum = a formal authoritative saying. From Latin *dictum*
innate = in from birth. From Latin *in* ... in + *nasci* ... to be born
stodge = a thick, dull food
vitiated = spoilt. From Latin *vitium* ... a vice

XI

Is you is or is you ain't my baby?

That fits the song but grammatically it's wrong.

There are good writers and good speakers who keep to the rules of English grammar without knowing them. They do well enough without rules because their ear was established in earliest childhood in their homes, where radio and television were intelligently supervised, and good language and good music were the norm. Consequently their taste was made incorruptible before they went to school. But such fortunates are in a tiny and dwindling minority. The great majority of young English-speakers are very much in need of lessons in grammar.

Amongst this majority, however, it is widely believed that care for grammar is a triviality fit only for pedant-bookworms, and that busy practical people (like themselves) need not be concerned with it. Of course, such anti-grammarites are unaware that some of history's celebrated men of action studied grammar carefully — Nelson, Wellington, Lincoln, Churchill, to name but a few of the English-speakers, and Julius Caesar for the ancient world, who actually wrote a treatise on Latin grammar.

Grammar is the science that states the rules governing the use of words in educated language. It does not make the rules,

---

dwindling = becoming smaller and smaller: wasting away
triviality = something of small value, little importance

but discovers them by analysing the ways by which the best writers and the best popular usage meet.

English grammar has seven important things called "parts of speech". They are noun, pronoun, adjective, preposition, conjunction, verb and adverb.

Noun – Name. The name of a person or thing. *Mary* is a good *girl*. Most *women* are good *cooks*. *Truth, beauty* and *happiness* cannot be touched, but they are real. Our *team* scored two *goals*.

Pronoun – Word used instead of a noun. Usually it enables one to go ahead without having to say the noun again.

James, Harry and Paul were at the party last night, and *they* drank too much. (*They* instead of repeating James, Harry and Paul) *Mine* is *this; yours* is *that. Who* is *that?* To *whom* are *you* writing? *I* love *you. He himself* will do *it*. (There the pronoun *himself* emphasizes the pronoun *he*) *One* ought not to treat *anybody* like *that. He* kissed *her. She* is pretty. *I* hope she loves *him*.

Adjective – Tells more about a noun or pronoun. *Lucky* you – *English* language – *Pretty* girl – She is *pretty* – *Dark* night – *Much* money – You are *lucky* – A *half* loaf – *Two* apples and *three* oranges – The *next* person – *My* book – *This* book (Remember that *this* was shown as a pronoun?] – *Her* apple (see *her* as a pronoun above) – The *best* time of the night – A *better* time of night – *Happy* John – *Sad* Joan is married to *happy* John – John is *happy*.

Preposition – shows what one noun or pronoun has to do with another.

The sky is *above* the earth. Run *up* the hill. ('You' understood) He stood *before* the gate. The cat sat *on* the mat. The book is *in* the case. Your car is *near* mine. (You) Please walk *around* the carpet, not *across* it. Flowers die *without* water. The boy fell *into* the water. A lion is *behind* you. The referee stood *between* the boxers. I want a dollar *for* this. *For* whom is this? This is *for* whom?

Conjunction – A word that joins one word or idea to another.

Jack *and* Jill – We wanted to leave, *but* our friends detained us, *and* we stayed another week in new York – He will do it, *or* they will do it – He went to bed, *for* he was feeling tired. (See *for* amongst the prepositions) – He says *that* his dinner is cold – He smiles *if* he is winning – They cannot do this *unless* you help them – He won the match *although* he was injured – Your coat is warmer *than* his (coat is) – He fell *because* he was ill.

Verb – A word (or more than one word) that shows action or a state of being.

The dog *bit* the man – The man *collapsed* – The woman *will hit* the dog – She *will sleep* first – "How I *hate* dogs!" *shouted* the woman – John *kicked* the ball – The ball *was kicked* by John. John *was* happy but *is* now sad. (The verbs point at his states of being)

Adverb – Adds meaning to verbs, adjectives, prepositions, conjunctions, and other adverbs.

He spoke *softly*. (Adds to the verb 'spoke') She is *very* beautiful. (Adds to the adjective 'beautiful') He swam *half* across the river. (Adds to the preposition 'across'. Note that *half* was an adjective further back) – He was respected *merely* because he could dance. (Adds to the conjunction 'because') – He spoke *very* softly. (Adds to the adverb 'softly')

MORE ABOUT THE VERB

It is the most important part of a statement. As you see from

> John *loves* Jane
> John *hates* Jane
> John *kissed* Jane
> John *killed* Jane

everything hinges on it.

Verbs show three things:

(i) Time (called TENSE from Latin *tempus* . . . time)

(ii) Manner of Speaking (called MOOD from Latin *modus* .. mood) and

(iii) Direction of the Action. Whether the main noun or pronoun (called the Subject) does the action or receives it. This index form of the verb is called its VOICE. There are two voices, *active* and *passive*. ('passive' = unresisting)

(i) TENSE

There are three tenses – past, present, and future: I *jumped*. (past) I *jump*. (present) I *shall jump*. (future)

(ii) MOOD

Mood is an Old English word. It means a frame of mind or state of feeling.

There are three moods, because you have three different manners of speaking, and you show these manners or 'moods' through verbs.

The first mood (INDICATIVE, from Latin *indicare* ... to point out) points out something as a fact. Most of what you say is in this mood.

He *jumped*. I *like* beer. I *go* to church.

The second mood (IMPERATIVE, from Latin *imperativus* ... commanding) carries a command or strong request:

You! *Jump*! *Go* to your room immediately.

The third mood (SUBJUNCTIVE, from latin *subjunctivus* ... joining on at the end as a yoke) gives neither fact nor command, but supposition, proposal, imagination, hopes, wishes — i.e., uncertain conditions. It can also express through the verb *be* an extreme formality. Think of such verbs as yoking an untrue or uncertain condition to a statement. The main verbs for signalling those conditions are *be* – *were* – *may*. The conjunctions 'if' and 'that' may also be signals of a subjunctive tc

---

yoke = a frame fitted around the necks of a pair of oxen or other working beasts in order tc harness them together; something that binds together

come. I suppose if I *were* to jump, I should jump onto you. (Supposition)

I propose that he *go* to Japan. (Proposal)

Let us imagine he *were* an elephant, and I *were* a butterfly. (Imagination)

May you both *be* happy all your lives. (Hope)

I wish I *were* a rich man. (Hope)

Notice that *were,* which in the other moods is a signal of past time, here carries no past. It is this unusual use of *were* with present and future, and its being attached to singular as well as plural nouns and pronouns that most clearly signals "SUBJUNCTIVE".

Here are more subjunctives:

(*May*) God *save* our gracious Queen.

(*May*) Heaven *forbid!*

Note that *May save* & *May forbid* are each one verb despite being separated

And though he *promise* to his loss,
He makes his promise good.
TATE & BRADY. Psalm XV. 5.

Though he *slay* me, yet will I trust in him: but I will maintain mine own ways before him.

JOB XIII. 15. King James Bible.

In indicative mood the last two examples would read: And though he *promises* to his loss ... Though he *slays* me ... Hence a verb shortened to its basic (no 's') in such constructions is a sign of subjunctive.

An example of subjunctive in extreme formality: I move that the motion *be approved.*

(iii) VOICE

The two voices of a verb:

ACTIVE:	The boy (Subject) *hit* the ball.
PASSIVE:	The ball (Subject) *was hit* by the boy.
PASSIVE:	The boy (Subject) *was hit* by the ball.
ACTIVE:	The ball (Subject) *hit* the boy.

(99)

97

VERBS continued

Obviously, in 'I *am jumping*' the jumping is still going on as the speaker speaks, and in 'I *had jumped*' it had ended. Each action has different degrees of completeness. There are four different degrees of completeness for each tense. Follow them through each tense.

Past Tense

(i)   I *jumped*. INDEFINITE simple. 'Indefinite' because the completeness of the action is not quite clear. 'Simple' = single. (There is only one word in the verb)

(ii) I *was jumping*. CONTINUOUS = going on without a break.

(iii) I *had jumped*. PERFECT = complete, finished. Some grammarians call the perfect in this tense PLUPERFECT = past ⑪⑱ perfect.

(iv) I *had been jumping*. PERFECT CONTINUOUS.

Present Tense

(i)   I *jump*. INDEFINITE SIMPLE.

(ii) I *am jumping*. CONTINUOUS.

(iii) I *have jumped*. PERFECT. (The action was finished before the moment of speaking)

(iv) I *have been jumping*. PERFECT CONTINUOUS.

Future Tense

Note

⑥⑦ *Shall, will, should, would* are amongst a small number of verbs that help other verbs to express mood and tense. They are called AUXILIARIES (from Latin *auxilium* ... help). *Am, was, have, had, be, been* are also auxiliaries that are on this and the next page.

(i)   I *shall* (or *will*) *jump*. INDEFINITE.

(ii) I *shall* (or *will*) *be jumping*. CONTINUOUS.

(iii) I *shall/will have jumped*. PERFECT. (The action will be finished in the future)

(iv) I shall/will have been jumping. PERFECT CONTINUOUS
(The 'been jumping' will have been finished)

Future in the Past

This tense describes action which <u>at some past time</u> was viewed as future. It is also the tense of reported speech.

  (i) I *thought* I *should jump.* INDEFINITE.
 (ii) I *said* I *should be jumping.* CONTINUOUS.
(iii) I *told* you I *should have jumped.* PERFECT.
 (iv) I *shouted* "I *should have been jumping".* PERFECT CONTINUOUS.

Further back I said 'There are three tenses — past, present, and future,' yet I have shown an extra tense. Consider that fourth tense not a main tense, but a mixture of two mains, Future and Past. At a later stage I shall show some of the nuances that mixtures of tense, mood and voice can give.

  Be clear that the labels Indefinite, Continuous, Perfect, and Perfect Continuous have nothing to do with time: they apply ⑰ only to the degree of completeness of an action that could be at any time. It is the tense that gives the time.

SENTENCES

(Sentence, from Latin *sententia* ... meaning)

A sentence is the complete expression of a thought: it says something clearly about a *subject*, which is always a noun or ⑨⑦ noun equivalent. What it says about the subject is its *predicate*. (from Latin *praedicare* ... to proclaim)

Subject	Predicate
John	sleeps
Time	flies
A sentence	is the complete expression of a thought
It	says something clearly about a subject

99

Every sentence must have a subject and a verb. The four verbs in the examples above are *sleeps, flies, is* and *says*.

"*Jump!*"
Is that a sentence? Yes, it is. Where is its subject? Its subject is '*You*', which is understood. (*You*, jump!)

The Two Steps to Finding the Subject of a Sentence

(i)   Find the verb.
(ii) Immediately *before* it ask "Who?" or "What?"
      Who sleeps? Answer: John. John = Subject.
      What flies? Answer: Time. Time = Subject.
      What is? Answer: A sentence. A sentence = Subject.
      What says? Answer: It. It = Subject.

(124) Now try step (ii) of the method on the following two sentences, and only after you have decided on your answer look at the correct answer at the end of this chapter. The verbs to be questioned are in italics.

1. The big red bus and the noisy old car *raced* down the road.
2. Early to bed and early to rise *makes* a man healthy, wealthy and wise.

Clause

Here are three sentences:

> I spoke. He ordered silence. I ground my teeth with rage.

Here they are in a single sentence:

> I spoke, but he ordered silence, and I ground my teeth with rage.

In making the long sentence the three short sentences have become *clauses*. A clause is a sentence within a sentence, and therefore every clause has a subject and a predicate. (Remember that every predicate has at least one verb)

The most natural and therefore the usual way of English is to have the subject at the beginning of a sentence with its verb following it, as in my examples so far. In this form it is easy to see that the subject is boss of a sentence, and you are unlikely to break a cardinal rule of English grammar namely, that <u>verb must agree with subject in NUMBER</u> (whether the verb is singular or plural) <u>and PERSON</u> (the verb must be given the right pronoun as its subject). You, not being a newcomer to English, do not have to be taught that the following are wrong:

The cat are
The cats is } faulty <u>number</u> in the verbs

Him hit
Them hit } faulty <u>person</u> in the pronouns
Me went

However, for good reasons to do with style, the subject is not always at the beginning of its sentence, and may even be preceded by its verb. It is in such unusual constructions that mistakes are more likely to be made. Here are such sentences:

Down, towards the mist in the valley went *the wounded animal*.

Subject of the verb 'went' = the wounded animal. Proof that "the wounded animal" is the subject is that it can stand at the beginning of the sentence without changing the sentence's meaning – "The wounded animal went down..." But such proof is unnecessary if you follow the simple two-step method of subject finding.

Here is a rule that must be applied to the next three examples: <u>In analysis all sentences are treated as assertions,</u> i.e., there are no questions, wishes or exclamations in analysis. "Can you do that?" becomes "You can do that". (Subject of verb 'can do' = you) "May he live long!" becomes "He may live long". (Subject of verb 'may live' = he) "How beautiful she is!" becomes "She is how beautiful". (Subject of verb 'is' = she)

Clause continued

A clause being a sentence within a sentence, for analysis it is treated as a sentence.

There are four kinds of clauses: main clause, and three kinds of subordinate clauses. The subordinates are equivalents of a noun, an adjective, or an adverb.

A main clause can stand on its own, i.e., it makes a sensible sentence quite apart from the sentence it is in. In the example under 'Clause' on page 79, each of the three clauses is a main clause. Here are five main clauses (each in italics):

> *He spoke,* and *I ground my teeth with rage.* (Two or more main clauses in a sentence are called CO-ORDINATE CLAUSES)
> *Show him* what you did. (The subject of the main clause is 'You' understood)
> *The man* that stole the money *has left.* (Main clause: The man has left)
> *I shall not leave* until he pays me.

The following are always subordinate clauses:

Noun clause. Each of the four is in italics.
Show him *what you did.* (Think of 'what you did' as a *thing*)
Whatever you do, do it now.
That he will do it is doubtful. (Main clause: (It) is doubtful)
I know *that you are ill.*

Adjective clause:
The man *who stole the money* has left. (Describes 'man')
The bus *that looked so bright and new* could not be started.
This is not the bread *that I bought.*
I found it in the cupboard *where I had left it.*

Every adjective clause tells about some noun or pronoun of some other clause.

Adverb clause:
I shall not leave *until he pays me.* (Throws light on the verb 'leave')

He spoke so softly *that nobody heard him.* (Throws light on the adverb 'softly')

I dug the hole *where you wanted it.* (Tells about *place*)

Because he was late, he missed the bus. (Gives *cause* or *reason*)

An adverb clause puts *time, place, reason* or *result* on some other clause. In the first sentence it puts time onto the main clause 'I shall not leave', and in the second it gives the result of 'He spoke so softly'.

More about adverb clauses later.

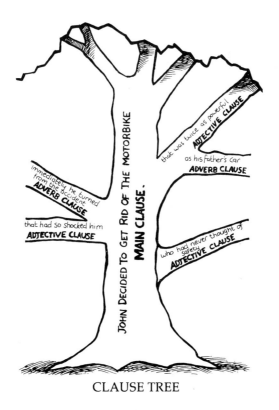

CLAUSE TREE

Immediately he turned from the accident that had so shocked him, John, who had never thought of safety, decided to get rid of the motorbike that was twice as powerful as his father's car.

103

Every sentence has a subject. Most sentences also have an OBJECT. An object (from Latin *objectus* ... a placing against) is a noun or noun-equivalent *towards* which a verb acts. Its usual place is after the verb.

> The dog bit *John*. (Object = John)
> He spelt *the word* correctly. (Object = the word)
> She wrote *a letter*. (Object = a letter)

It is easy to see that in those sentences the objects *received* direct action from the subjects through the verbs.

An object may be a clause:

The teacher said *that the boy was lazy*. (Object of the verb 'said' = the noun clause, which is in italics)

The above are all **direct objects**: their verbs act directly upon them.

The Two Steps to Finding the Direct Object of a Sentence

(i)   Find the verb.

(ii) Immediately *after* it ask 'What?' or 'Whom?' (If you ask it 'Who?' I hope it jumps out of the sentence and bites you) ⑦⑥ ⑩ Bit whom? Answer: John = Direct object. Spelt what? Answer: The word = Direct Object. Wrote what? Answer: a letter = Direct Object. Said what? Answer: that the boy was lazy = Direct object.

Do not confuse this method with that of finding the subject. Their respective keys are *after* and *before*.

Many sentences have an **INDIRECT OBJECT**. This is clearly less important than the direct object, which of course is in the same sentence.

> She wrote *me* a letter. (Indirect Object = me)
> I gave *him* a present. (Indirect Object = him)
> The Roman father taught *his son* manners. (Indirect Object = his son)
> He poured *John* a drink. (Indirect Object = John)

Generally in English sentences, indirect object *precedes* direct object, as in the above sentences.

The Two Steps to Finding the Indirect Object of a Sentence

(i) Find the verb.
(ii) Immediately after it ask 'To whom? To what?' or 'For whom? For What?'. Wrote *to* whom? Answer: me = Indirect Object. Gave *to* whom? Answer: him = Indirect Object. Taught *to* whom? Answer: his son = Indirect Object. Poured *for* whom? Answer: John = Indirect Object.

You see that the indirect object has fundamental meanings that are in *to* and *for*. Hence, one of those prepositions can be put into a sentence that has an indirect object:

She wrote a letter *to* me. I gave a present *to* him. The Roman father taught manners *to* his son. He poured a drink *for* John.
Note that when the prepositions are put in, the indirect objects come immediately after them, and the sentence order is changed from

Verb – Indirect Object – Direct Object
to
Verb – Direct Object – Indirect Object

(104) (76)

Further to what I said about *who* & *whom* on page 75, I trust that you now see their grammatical (and logical) foundation: *who* always signals Subject, and *whom* Object —— helpful signals in an involved sentence. By the same principle *I* is always (4) Subject, and *me* always Object or Indirect Object.

I hit John.	John hit *me*.
This is the great Chiron *who* Achilles nursed. [Chiron was the nurse]	This is the great Chiron *whom* Achilles nursed. [Achilles was the nurse]

Still More About Verbs

There are three verbal states —— (i) TRANSITIVE, (ii) IN-TRANSITIVE, and (iii) LINKING. A verb in the first state must have an object. Verbs in the other states cannot have objects. Only in the first state can a verb have voice, ie. be active or passive.

(i) Transitive

(From Latin *trans* ... across + *ire* ... go – *transire* ... to go across)

In Active Voice the verb carries the action from Subject to Object

thus

SUBJECT	action		OBJECT
The dog	bit	⟶	John

In Passive Voice the verb carries the action from Object to Subject

thus

SUBJECT	action		OBJECT
John	⟵ was bitten	by	the dog

SUBJECT   OBJECT
John *bit* the dog. (Active)

SUBJECT   OBJECT
The dog *was bitten* by John (Passive)

In those two sentences the meanings are the same, but Subject and Object have been reversed. The same applies to the following pairs.

SUBJECT   OBJECT
He *played* the game. (Active)

SUBJECT   OBJECT
The game *was played* by him. (Passive)

SUBJECT   OBJECT
He *spelt* the word. (Active)

SUBJECT   OBJECT
The word *was spelt* by him. (Passive)

(ii) Intransitive

(Latin *in* ... not)

In this state a verb carries no action from its subject. Hence it needs no object. With its subject it makes a complete statement. As it is not active it cannot be made passive.

> SUBJECT
> His illness *grew* worse.
>
> SUBJECT
> The dog *bites.*
>
> SUBJECT
> John *cried.*
>
> SUBJECT
> He *played* well.

As you will have seen from the examples – some verbs can change from one state to the other. Indeed, most English verbs may be made transitive or intransitive to fit the context.

> He *played* the game well. (Transitive)
> He *played* well. (Intransitive)

(ii) Linking

A linking verb is really a kind of intransitive.

It has no voice, i.e. it carries no action, and merely links the subject to information about itself. It differs from intransitives proper in requiring another word or words after it to make sense. In proper intransitives such as 'He ran', 'He slept', the verbs complete a meaning, but in 'The sea *is*', the linking verb 'is' cannot form a complete predicate on its own: it is only a link from subject to predicate and more is required. The more that is required is its COMPLEMENT (from Latin *complere*. ... to finish, to fill up) . The most common linking verbs are: am, is, are, was, be, been, got, get, were. These are all forms of the verb TO BE, i.e. *to be completed.* Some other linking verbs are: ap-

pears, looks, tastes, feels. Those last four can also be transitive.
(She *feels* the material)

The sea *is* deep. (Complement is an adjective)
Love *is* blind. (Complement is an adjective)
Time *is* money (Complement is a noun)
God *is* love. (Complement is a noun)
Who *am* I? (Complement is a pronoun)
It *is* I. (Complement is a pronoun)
It *is* he. (Complement is a pronoun)

None of those sentences has an Object. That is because their
verbs and complements arc stuck to their subjects, so that with
the nouns and pronouns of their complements

SUBJECT	=	COMPLEMENT
Time	=	money
Money	=	time
Who	=	I
I	=	who
It	=	he
He	=	it

In mathematical reasoning, if SUBJECT = COMPLEMENT,
COMPLEMENT = SUBJECT. So, pronouns that show the Object of a sentence (him, her, me, them, us) are wrong after verbs
'to be'.

MORE ABOUT CLAUSES

You have been given most of what you need to know about
main clauses, noun clauses and adjective clauses, but a lot more
must be said about adverb clauses, because there are no fewer
than ten of them, each showing one of the following things:
(Each example consists of a main clause and an adverb clause:
the latter is in italics)

(1) Time

I shall not leave *until he pays me.* (Conjunction: until)
I shall leave *before he pays me.* (Conjunction: before)
I shall leave *after he pays me.* (Conjunction: after)
I shall leave *immediately he pays me.* (Conjunction: immediately.
Here it is an adverb acting as a conjunction)

(2) Place

I dug the hole *where you wanted it.* (Conjunction: where. Here it
is an adverb acting as a conjunction)

I shall dig the hole *wherever you want it.* (Conjunction: wherever)

(3) Reason

I dug the hole *because you needed it.* (Conjunction: because)
Since you are not honest, I must dissolve the partnership. (Con-
junction: Since)
As you are not ready, we must leave without you. (Conjunction:
As)

(4) Manner

Do it *as you think best.* (Conjunction: as)
He covered her eyes *so that she should not see the terrible deed.*
(Conjunction: so that. Here 'so' is an adverb acting with 'that'
to form a conjunction)

(5) Cause

Because he was late he missed the bus. (Conjunction: Because)
I am glad *that you are well.* (Conjunction: that)

(6) Concession (or Contrast)

He lost *though he did his best.* (Conjunction: though)

Although Mount Rupert is higher, Mount Grey is more difficult to climb. (Conjunction: Although)

(7) Condition

If you do not hurry you will be late. (Conjunction: If)
I will do this *if you do that*. (Conjunction: if)
Unless you do that, I shall not do this. (Conjunction: Unless)

(8) Purpose

I eat *(so) that I may live*. (Conjunction: that)
I eat *lest I should die*. (Conjunction: lest)
I removed them *so that the children should not be frightened*. (Conjunction: so that)

(9) Result (or Effect)

He worked so hard *that the job was finished within a week*. (Conjunction: that)
He left so late *that he missed the train*. (Conjunction: that)

Notice that this clause and the previous one use the same binary conjunction *so that*, but in Clause of Purpose the *so* and the *that* are generally side by side, whereas in Clause of Result they are generally separated by an intervening word. The main difference between these clauses, however, is in MOOD, Clause of Purpose being Subjunctive, and Clause of Result being Indicative.

(10) Comparison

She is shorter *than I am (short)*. (Conjunction: than)
John is taller *than his brother (is tall)*. (Conjunction: than)
John is taller *than his brother was (tall) at that age*. Conjunction: than)
He does not love you *as much as I do (love you)*. (Conjunction: as)

Clause-mnemonics for Those Preparing for English Examinations

Remember that the following conjunctions go with the clauses shown:

and – or – nor – but – for	CO-ORDINATE CLAUSE
though – although	CLAUSE OF CONCESSION
if – unless	CLAUSE OF CONDITION
lest – so that	CLAUSE OF PURPOSE
so ... that	CLAUSE OF RESULT

The first signal of this last clause is the adverb *so,* which is in the MAIN CLAUSE. This *so* then combines with the *that* of the following clause to make this type of conjunction.

than – as	CLAUSE OF COMPARISON

The main thing to bear in mind about this clause is that its verb and adjective are often omitted. Another point to bear in mind is that sometimes, in speaking, the correct grammar in this clause makes it sound pedantic: She is shorter than I, has this disability. The remedy is simple: include the verb – She is shorter than I *am* – sounds easy, and it is grammatically correct, far better than the bad grammar of She is shorter than me. Be clear though that that remedy is only for sentences in which "I" is compared. Verbal or adjectival addition to most other Comparison Clauses makes them grossly unidiomatic as in

John is taller than his brother *is* (or *is tall*)

and

John is taller than his brother was *tall* at his age.

Clauses of Time, Place, Reason, Manner, and Cause are so clear in sense as to need no mnemonics.

---

mnemonics = a trick for helping the memory. From Greek *mnasthai* ... to remember

111

YET MORE ABOUT CLAUSES

Splitting

You have seen that a verb may be split. So may clauses. The *main clause* 'The bus could not be started' was split by an adjective clause as follows: *The bus,* which looked so bright and new, *could not be started.* Here is a *noun clause* split by an adjective clause:

The doctor said *that the man* who had been injured *died last night.*

Here is an *adverb clause* with an intervening adjective clause:

He spoke so loudly *that Jack,* who was dozing at the door, *heard him.*

Ellipsis = an omission that is readily understood from the context.

(You call) Socrates a fool! You (are an) idiot! Each statement is a sentence.

There was no one there but I (was there). Two co-ordinate clauses.

I hope (that it is) not (so). Noun clause has the ellipses.

His enemies, though (they have been) beaten, are still dangerous. Clause of Concession has the ellipsis.

If (it is) possible, (you should) come early. Both the Main Clause and the Clause of Condition have an ellipsis.

Abridgement (from Latin *abbreviare . . .* to make short)

Ellipsis does not make a fundamental change, but abridgement does, and it does so through types of verbs that have not yet been explained in this booklet. Explanations will follow the examples.

In the following examples, types of clauses that have already been given will be abridged by NON-FINITE verbs. The fundamental change is that a non-finite verb *does away with a clause* by taking the place of its finite verb, and thus turns the clause into a *phrase.* The non-finite verbs in the following are in italics.

112

CLAUSE OF CONDITION

We shall go, if the weather permits.

PARTICIPLE

We shall go, weather *permitting*.

CLAUSE OF REASON

As I was ill,   I stayed at home.

PARTICIPLE

Being ill, I stayed at home.

CLAUSE OF TIME

After I had finished my work, I had a cup of coffee.

PARTICIPLE

Having finished my work I had a cup of coffee.

NOUN CLAUSE

It is stupid of you that you should say it.

INFINITIVE

It is stupid of you   *to say*   it.

GERUND

Your *saying* it is stupid.

CLAUSE OF TIME

I was surprised when I saw this.

INFINITIVE

I was surprised   *to see*   this.

NON-FINITE VERBS

So far the verbs exampled under VERBS have been FINITE (from Latin *finitus* ... bounded, limited). Finite verbs are tied to number, person, tense, subject and predicate. The finite verb 'go' for example is tied to present tense and the persons of I, They, We and You, so that you may not say He go – She go – It go – or He goed, but you must change its form as follows: He goes – She goes – It goes – and, for its past tense in a single word – He went.

As you saw from the examples in Abridgement, NON-FI-NITE verbs (from Latin *infinitus* ... boundless) can compress clauses into phrases without any loss of meaning or force. By giving English simpler and shorter routes to meaning they have conferred an incomparable blessing on the language.

There are three non-finite verbs: participle, gerund and infinitive.

Participle (from latin *pars* ... a part + *capere* ... to take)

It grew from a verb and has taken to itself adjective qualities. It thus has a mixed character, part verb, part adjective.

Verbal Force	**Adjectival Force**
It is *jumping*.	*It is a jumping* animal.
He is *loving*. (ACTIVE)	He is a *loving* person.
He is *being loved*. (PASSIVE)	
He was *loved*. (PAST TENSE)	

Gerund (or Verbal Noun)

It grew from a verb and has taken to itself noun qualities. It always ends in -ing, and therefore has the same form as a present participle. It expresses an action or a happening in general terms without reference to Time or Name. Think of a gerund as a thing.

Jumping is good for you. He likes *jumping*. I like his *jumping*. To build upon any other foundation is *building* upon sand. I rejoiced at his *jumping*.

The following may look like present participles, but, as you see from their meanings, they are gerunds: *knitting*-needle = a needle for *knitting* - *writing*-desk = a desk for *writing*.

Infinitive

'Infinitive' is a misleading term for those constructions: infinitives are not more infinitive than participles or gerunds. Their function is similar to that of gerunds, but they are more focussed. They are generally coupled with gerunds when there are two actions in an event, with the gerund bearing less of the weight: To *build* upon any other foundation is building upon sand.

To *jump* is good for you. He likes to *jump*. I should like to *see* you.

Most infinitives are preceded by 'to', but there are many that are not: You need not *send* (*to send*) the files to him.

*   *   *   *

Over hundreds of years English has been a good instrument of communication because it has adapted efficiently to the different intellectual requirements of each generation, with its best changes always towards quicker, simpler expression. Central to this evolving efficiency are prepositions, and non-finite verbs. Here are typical mistakes with non-finite verbs.

PARTICIPLE MISTAKES
(Participles are in italics)

P A R T I C I P L E   P H R A S E
Rushing down the mountain with a terrible roar, he saw the wall of water.

But it was the wall of water, not he, that was *rushing* down the mountain with a terrible roar. That was therefore a MISRE-LATED PARTICIPLE PHRASE. Recast correctly: He saw the wall of water, which was *rushing* down the mountain...

P A R T I C I P L E   P H R A S E
Having been badly *defeated* last week, there is little likelihood of his having a better result this week.

That participle phrase lacks relation to any noun or pronoun. It is an UNRELATED PARTICIPLE PHRASE. Recast: As he *was* badly *defeated* last week, there is little likelihood of his having a better result this week. (*Was defeated* is a past participle)

Rules against misrelated and unrelated participle phrases: <u>Keep the participle phrase as near as possible to the noun or pronoun to which it is related in sense.</u> This means that that related noun or pronoun should generally come within the

115

participle phrase or right after it. Clearly, that general rule is based as much on commonsense as on grammar.

It does not apply to a type of participle phrase called ABSOLUTE, because such a phrase is considered to be grammatically independent of the clause that follows it: the participle of the absolute-phrase refers only to the noun or pronoun *within* the phrase, and that noun or pronoun is regarded as the subject of the phrase, not of the sentence:

Absolute Phrase

The city *taken*, . . .	Caesar set out for Rome.
Weather *permitting*, . . .	the finals will be on Saturday.
The cook *being* absent, . . .	no dinner was prepared.
The gunman *being disarmed* and behind bars, . . .	the sheriff could enjoy his coffee.

Rule: <u>There should be no commas within an Absolute Phrase.</u>

The gunman, *being disarmed* and behind bars, . . .

The rest of that sentence must now tell about the *gunman*, else it forms a MISRELATED PARTICIPLE PHRASE.

Absolute-Phrases are equivalent to adverb clauses, as can be seen if one turns them into clauses:

When the city was taken . . . CLAUSE OF TIME
If the weather permits . . . CLAUSE OF CONDITION
Because the cook was absent . . . CLAUSE OF REASON

MISTAKES WITH GERUNDS
(Gerunds are in italics)

I watched John ^{Participle} jumping.

I watched John's ^{Gerund} *jumping*.

Both those sentences are correct, but their meanings are different. In the first, my attention is on John: it was Jumping John that I watched. In the second sentence my attention is on the jumping, and John is secondary.

If you remember that a gerund should be thought of as a thing (because it has noun quality), you will have no doubt that the following are wrong:

That was the cause of us *losing* the match.
You must prevent him *leaving*.
You must forbid him *coming*.

Those sentences should have:

our *losing*,
his *leaving*,
his *coming*.

Such mistakes are due to the speaker's confusing the gerund with the participle. They are stigmatised as FUSED PARTI-CIPLES in Fowler's MODERN ENGLISH USAGE.

Rule: A gerund may be preceded by 'the' (the *coming* of the enemy), by 'a' (a *coming* that brought misery), by a preposition (What about *jumping*?), by a possessive adjective (our, his, my, their, your *coming*), or by a genitive, i.e. a noun turned into a signal of possession (John's *jumping*) – in short, by any word that can precede a noun or pronoun, but it should never be preceded by a personal pronoun (us, him, me, them, you).

INFINITIVE MISTAKES

There are four: too much perfect, incorrect relation, split infini-tive, and wrong idiom.

(99) **(i) Too much perfect with certain verbs**

Notice that 'have' and 'had' signal Perfect and Pluperfect re-spectively.

X PERFECT PERFECT INFINITIVE
I should have liked *to have been* there.

✓ PERFECT PRESENT INFINITIVE
I should have liked *to be* there.

✓ PRESENT or FUTURE INDEFINITE   PERFECT INFINITIVE
I should like *to have been* there = Now (at this moment) *or*
At a future time I wish I had been at that past event.

✓ PRESENT or FUTURE INDEFINITE   PRESENT INFINITIVE
I should like *to be* there. = Now (at this moment) *or* At a
future time I want to be there. The context would point at
the time intended.

X PLUPERFECT   PERFECT INFINITIVE
I had intended *to have seen* him in London.

✓ PLUPERFECT   PRESENT INFINITIVE
I had intended *to see* him in London.

✓ SIMPLE PAST   PRESENT INFINITIVE
I intended *to see* him in London.

X SIMPLE PAST   PERFECT INFINITIVE
I intended *to have seen* him in London.

The logic of such constructions is that they show two *separate*
times, with the Present Infinitive always *further into the future
than the finite verb.*

118

Notice also the idea of non-attainment that 'have' and 'had' can carry: 'I should have liked' means that what I wanted I never got.

Rule: <u>When the infinitive is the *object* of the following past tense verbs</u>

attempted	hoped	started
began	intended	tried
ceased	learnt	used
commenced	liked	wanted
continued	longed	wished
decided	loved	
desired	meant	
expected	preferred	
feared	prepared	
	proposed	

<u>it must be in the Present</u>.

Addendum

PAST   PERFECT INFINITIVE

I was astonished *to have won.*

PERFECT INFINITIVE

He considered the matter *to have been settled.*

Do those sentences not invalidate the rule? They do not. I have said it before, and I say it again: Grammar is based on logic and commonsense. In the first sentence the astonishment and the winning were at the same time: *to have won* acts immediately as an adverb on the verb 'was astonished'. 'Astonished' is not on the list of verbs in the rule. In the second sentence the Perfect Infinitive points at an action that took place *before* the action of the main verb. 'Considered' is not on the list of verbs in the rule.

addendum = thing to be added (plural addenda). Pure Latin

Those who would take their knowledge of Infinitives to an advanced level could not do better than study this fascinating aspect of English in C.T. Onions' MODERN ENGLISH SYNTAX, and G.O. Curme's ENGLISH GRAMMAR.

(ii) Split Infinitives

I want you *to* gently and carefully *pack* the glasses into the box.
Rather

I want you *to pack* the glasses into the box gently and carefully.

General Rule: <u>Do not separate *to* from its infinitive.</u>

The reason behind that rule is that a split infinitive is a *weakened* infinitive. Comparison of the two examples will show that not only is the infinitive in the first sentence weakened, but so also are the adverbs 'gently' and 'carefully', whereas in the second sentence the two ideas — packing, and method of packing — by being kept unmingled, build a more robust statement.

There are contexts, however, where a split infinitive is unavoidable or stylistically preferable:

Will you ask John *to* kindly *tell* the baker to call on Monday.

(Put 'kindly' in front of 'to' and you change the meaning)

The same remark applies to such as *to* more than *double*, and *to* better *equip*. As to style, there is no changing Robert Herrick's split infinitive in TO THE LARK.

> Good speed, for I this day
> Betimes my matins say,
> Because I do
> Begin to woo.
> Sweet singing lark,
> Be thou the clerk,

betimes = early; in good time
Herrick, Robert (1591–1674) A friend of Ben Jonson's. The Victorian poet and critic Swinburne thought him 'the greatest song-writer ever born of English race'
Matins = morning prayers in the Church of England. From Latin *matutinus* ... of the morning
woo = to court a woman with a view to marriage

And know thy when
To say Amen.
And if I prove
Blest in my love,
Then thou shalt be
High Priest to me,
At my return
To incense *burn,*
and so to solemnize
Love's and my sacrifice.

So — if you break the General Rule, you should do so with commonsense and a good ear.

Rule: If you are unsure, do not separate the infinitive from its 'to'.

(iii) Idiomatic blunder

When infinitive is used instead of gerund:

X √

I cannot avoid *to see* him   I cannot avoid seeing him

He cannot give up *to smoke*   He cannot give up smoking

MORE ABOUT PREPOSITIONS

The Old English (Anglo-Saxon) of more than twelve hundred years ago was nowhere near as supple as Modern English, mainly because it lacked many prepositions and had therefore to rely on adverbs, changeable word endings (inflexions), and proximity of one noun to another in the word-order. The prox-

---

incense = spices that give sweet-smelling smoke while burning. Used in some ceremonies in the Church of England. From Latin *in* ... in + *candere* ... to burn

solemnize = to go through a serious ritual such as a marriage ceremony. From Latin *sollus* . .. whole, entire

imity principle of that primitive language survives today in compound expressions such as *football* = a ball for the feet, *rat-trap* = a trap for rats, *tooth-brush* = a brush for teeth. In these compounds clarity is enhanced by *absence* of the preposition: as usual, English in its pragmatic trend towards perfection has taken the best from a general defect and left the inferior behind.

Most of the important prepositions were at first adverbs. That is why adverbs and prepositions are so closely related in English.

Examples:

Prepositions	Adverbs
We moved *along* the platform	Move *along* please
We walked *around* the field	The men stood *around*
He stood *before* the window	I have seen her once *before*
He stood *behind* her	Please walk *behind*
He hung *below* me	He hung *below*
By whom was this done?	The bus went *by*
The dead ox floated *down* the river	Please sit *down*
He waited *inside* the house	He is *inside*
Fish swim *in* the dam	He came *in*
It is spread *over* all the world	It spread all the world *over*

Phrases, those pithy expressions short of a clause that yet carry the meaning of a clause, are introduced by prepositions, or by non-finite verbs. Here are the types of phrases formed with prepositions: a lump *of* lead. Adjective phrase = a leaden lump
He is good *for* nothing. Adverb phrase
He stood *by* the window. Adverb phrase
There is every probability *of* his being defeated. Gerund phrase
He paused *for* her to reply. Infinitive phrase

---

pragmatic = dealing with events in the light of practical lessons; practical in outlook. From Greek *pragmatikos* ... practical; businesslike

compounded with certain intransitives, they turn them into transitives as follows:

speak *to* – depend *upon* – call *on* – laugh *at* – wish *for* – sleep *with* – think *of*. Indeed, the influence of those prepositions is so great that they must be thought of as part of the verb. So in 'He was waited for' *was waited for* is one verb.

SOME PREPOSITIONS WRONGLY USED

All the mistakes show an unidiomatic ear.

√	X
His success was *in* a great measure owing to his wife's talent	to
aim *at*	for
enamoured *of*	with
disgust *with*	at
different *from*	than
confronted *with*	by
free *from* worry	of
in respect *of*	to
judged *by* his performance	on
protest *against*	at
sparing *of* money	with
suffer *from* a broken leg	with
oblivious *of*	to

FINAL ABOUT LIKE & AS

Further to the general rule regarding *like* and *as*: *like* controls nouns and pronouns in the most simple way, and *as* controls clauses and phrases. Thus in 'She is *like* a bird', *like* simply compares as an adjective the pronoun *she* to the noun *bird;* and in 'Do *as* I tell you', *as* as a conjunction with adverbial force connects the clauses

	CLAUSE		CLAUSE
√	[You do]	*as*	[I tell you.]

One more illustration to clinch the matter:

√ He laughs *like* his father. (Here there is just a sentence with no clause after *like*)

√ He laughs *as* his father does. (Here addition of the verb 'does' makes a clause)

Therefore I hope that

X 'He laughs *like* his father does' sounds ugly to you,

and that you will improve

X It looks *like* it's been put together by many hands

to

√ It seems to have been put together by many hands.

Of course, when *like* is used as a *verb,* the foregoing rules do not apply:

√ I *like* you.
I *like* you when you smile.

Answer: The subjects are:

1. The big red bus and the noisy old car. 2. Early to bed and early to rise.

124

Appendix I

A FEW EXAMPLES OF DIFFERENCES BETWEEN BRITISH & AMERICAN ENGLISH

Idiom

American		British
Write Box 789	:	Write to Box 789
aim to make	:	aim at making

Spelling

color	:	colour
pajamas	:	pyjamas

Vocabulary

Argentinians	:	Argentines
bathtub	:	bath
crazy bone	:	funny bone
diaper	:	nappy
elevator	:	lift
fall	:	autumn
line	:	queue
a period	:	a full stop
vacation	:	holiday
witness stand	:	witness box
zero	:	nought

Yes—— to the glory and vitality of English, there are regional differences in English, but do not accept the sophism propagated by half-thinking academics and fully used by incompetents to gloze mistakes in their writing, that there are *different Englishes*, one as good as the other. British, American, Australian, South African are among their examples.

While it is obvious that English accents differ greatly; that some idioms differ slightly (in a minority of expressions); that spellings and meanings differ unimportantly for a few words

sophism = a simplicity made complex by false argument that is designed to give a wrong idea. From Latin *sophisma* ... clever device; trick [From Greek.]

125

———it is obvious to anybody who properly reads the best contemporary writings in English, that in the mainstream of *writing* there is only one English, and competent writers adhere to the principles of its grammar, syntax and vocabulary, and are easily understood by all educated English-speakers around the world.

---

adhere = keep fixed to. From Latin *ad* ... to + *haerere* ... to stick
syntax = the right order for words in sentences. From Greek *syn* ... together + *tassein* ... arrange

Appendix II

THE PROBLEM: HOW TO STOP THE DECLINE IN ENGLISH

When that problem is solved and proper action taken, the decline in general education in the English-speaking world will also be halted, because the quality of English directly affects the quality of all general education through English. That quality of language and quality of culture are inseparably joined together I take as self-evident.

Cause and effect relative to this problem being the same throughout the English-speaking world, its solution in one country will apply in any other.

Improvement should commence in Britain, because contamination at the fountain-head of English runs to every other English-speaking area, and improvement there will sooner or later show in the rest of the English-speaking world. Britain is of prime importance because, although its worst education is frightful, the standard of its *best* is the highest in the English-speaking world.

In Britain there is now growing acceptance that there are serious defects in the national education, and that most of them stem from bad English, but contrary to the sanguine expectation of some, that schools and universities can soon be drastically improved by stricter selection of teachers and increased salaries for them, I fear that the deterioration in most educational establishments is too far-gone for quick correction. To raise salaries is no solution. That would simply give incompetents extra money and enhanced status; and even if the best people were attracted to teaching, their minority influence amongst a vast mass of entrenched opinionated second-raters would take at least two generations to tell. In short, professors, headmasters and teachers who for years have accepted stupid dogma without demur can never be turned into respectable educators, and are certain to impede betterment.

The only practical instruments now for quick improvement are radio and television, and fortunately for all of us they are the most potent educative forces that Man has ever had. Their power to raise either good or bad taste is overwhelming—— overwhelming because they lay the foundations of musical and literary taste in the large majority of our children long before they go to school. Broadcasting thus dominates our culture.

I come of a tennising family. In all my life up to the 1974 Wimbledon Championship I heard no grunts on a tennis court. By 1975 almost every keen child player that I saw grunted when serving, and this happened on tennis courts around the world for a number of years in emulation of Jimmy Connors, whose grunting at Wimbledon was on radio and television.

No implication that grunting in tennis is bad: I merely exemplify the sway of broadcasting.

More than two hundred years ago a wise Scot said that, ". . . if a man were permitted to make all the ballads, he need not care who should make the laws of a nation".

The general standard of ballads in English in olden times was incomparably higher than it is today. This was because their lyrics and music had to stand the test of a public approbation that was not pushed and manipulated by a huge advertising industry; and it was not just the young that formed the sieve of popular judgment, but the older, more experienced part of the population as well. Narrative ballads and love songs that became popular in the old days thus touched the feelings of the unlettered folk for whom they were made, as well as the most learned and discriminating of the community.

Today pop-song is the balladry of the English-speaking world. It is produced by a shrewd, highly efficient recording industry that aims its advertising exclusively at the young. What is raised to "Number One Smash Hit of the Month" rises more by advertising on the wings of broadcasting than by artistic merit. Although there are a few pop songs of beauty and sincerity every year amongst the welter, they are such a tiny fraction of total production that they can do nothing to affect mass taste.

Truth is, most copywriters in advertising have taste inferior to that of a good creative writer, but the great wealth and hyperbolizing style of the industry coupled with the even lower aesthetic taste of its paymasters in commerce and industry have boosted advertising to a mighty power for glorifying the inferior. For the broad mass of English-speakers, advertising is now the predominant influencer of their culture. The stock older child may read a classic as a school setwork, but he talks and *thinks* in the cliche of pop-lyric and advertising. He may (if he is above average) know that Bach and Shakespeare are supposed to be better than the current pop music and Dallas-type drama, but great art has never touched him and never will, because his natural potential for good taste was ruined in earliest childhood by a constant flood from broadcasting, of inferior music, inferior language, and inferior action. With pitiably few exceptions his teachers, priests and public functionaries now also act and speak according to the second-rate standard set by advertising and spread by broadcasting and, of course, so do his parents.

I believe that the music and lyrics of bad pop have done more to spoil our culture than bad schools; and the good radio and television produced by talented and dedicated broadcasters cannot tip the scale against this loud rubbish weighted by advertising. Those who think this an hysterical belief and themselves take no account of the *quality* of music and language that is forming children's taste should consider Plato's belief, endorsed by Aristotle, that in education musical training is a more potent instrument than any other, "because rhythm and harmony find their way into the inward places of the soul, on which they mightily fasten, imparting grace, and making the soul of him who is rightly educated graceful, or of him who is ill-educated ungraceful; and also because he who has received this true education of the inner being will most shrewdly perceive omissions or faults in art and nature, and with a true taste, while he praises and rejoices over and receives into his soul the good, and becomes noble and good, he will blame and hate the bad, now in the days of his youth, even before he is able to know the reason why". And the advice of Confucius:

"Let the character be formed by the poets: established by the laws of right behaviour; and perfected by music".

I imagine that wise Scot transported from the 17th century for a television viewing of a typical POP SHOP type of regular presentation for children and teenagers that may be seen in any English-speaking country, of the latest pop songs, and I guess that what would arouse his disgust first would be the uglification of young faces in routine ape-like contortion; then would follow disgust with the inane lyrics in bad English; and when he had come to his complete assessment without finding *any* point that was not coarse and ugly, I imagine him expressing his abhorrence to a venerable-looking grandfather and being told: "I don't like it, but who's to judge what's ugly? What can one do? They like it." Surely that Scot would conclude, even if he marvelled at our scientific and technological advances, that our civilization was diseased to the core.

This English-speaking disease has not been brought on by villainous cunning, but by the cult of the second-rate that has given oafs in relatively few positions the enormous power of instant mass influence —— especially on the young.

The remedy now can come only from broadcasting. Broadcasting can stop the decline in English. There will then be a seemingly miraculous cultural improvement. Proper steps taken to this end in Britain will soon influence not only the rest of the English-speaking world, but the host of non-English speakers around the world who use English.

THE SOLUTION

The BBC as the most influential broadcaster should set the example. Its example would have an immediate effect upon independent radio and television in Britain. This independent broadcasting is funded by advertising, and its advertisers would be forced by public opinion that had been sharpened by the BBC, to look more critically at themselves.

All regular BBC staff on production, announcing or commentating in English who are below first-rate should be weeded out, and only top-class replacements should be taken in. The main criterion should be ability in English. This criterion should, of course, apply to disc-jockeys and sports-commentators.

I am convinced that the BBC, despite the many highly talented and cultured servants that it has, is now unable to purge itself. That pockets of ignorance have been there so long continuously strengthening themselves, often aggressively, against the cultured, proves that the cultured within the BBC are not strong enough to stop the inward rot. For the following actions the whole weight of the British government coupled with public opinion will have to be thrown into the scale.

(1) The charter of the BBC should be withdrawn and a new charter given only after a satisfactory reorganization.

(2) A secretary of state for the BBC should be appointed to plan and oversee the reorganization.

(3) He should choose a committee of wise and culured advisors. At least two Americans should be invited to be on the committee.

(4) No member of the BBC should be on the committee.

(5) No member of any other broadcasting organization should be on the committee.

(6) Main entrance to employment in BBC broadcasting should be by a stiff annual competitive examination. The secretary of state for the BBC and his committee should plan its institution. Advice from broadcasters and journalists should, of course, be canvassed.

(7) One other entry to employment in broadcasting should be by the *collective* discretion of the board of governors of the BBC (all appointed by the secretary of state). This entry

would be for those that had already given proof of genius or high talent.

These actions, by drawing on the finest talents in Britain, would make the BBC the paramount and most worthy exemplar for the nation. Every school and university would be profoundly influenced. Soon ——— insincerity, unintelligence and bad English in advertisements would come to be spotted even by primary-school children, and advertising agencies would be forced to a weeding.

To the inevitable criticism that the bulk of the British do not like intellectualism, I reply that the new BBC of excellent discrimination would not need to be told that: all its light programmes, like the good old ballads, would be free from intellectual heaviness and preaching; there would be plenty of *good* pop music, and, especially in programmes for children and teenagers, good songs and dances from the past as well.

If the British government has the will to tackle the BBC, it has a fund of good precedent to guide it from the annals of a mighty mercantile company's connection with India.

Up to the last quarter of the 18th century the British East India Company was, by charter of the crown, the paramount ruler in India. Most of the company's British officials were honourable and efficient, but British reputation was tarnished by ineptitude and dishonesty of a minority. In consequence, the home government wisely curtailed more and more of the company's power and, finally, after the Indian Mutiny middle of last century, it assumed complete responsibility for governing its Indian empire. The worst officials of the company were discharged or retired, and the best retained as servants of the new British government in India. The crown of administrative excellence was finally achieved when competitive examination was made the sole entrance to the higher ranks of the Indian Civil Service.

The British government has one other rich fund to draw on: the good sense of the British people. If it puts the case for drastic action in a straightforward manner to the nation, I believe it will gain majority approval.

Bibliography

These books are all recommended. Those considered particularly suitable for further study of English have an *
  Books in this bibliography that are not recommended are at the end.

Abraham Lincoln: His Speeches and Writings. World Publishing, New York 1946

ALDERTON PINK, M. & THOMAS, S.E. *English Grammar, Composition and Correspondence.* The Dannington Press, St Albans 1963. A list of authors recommended for reading

American English/English American. Abson Books 1979. A two-way glossary of English

ARISTOTLE. *The Works of Aristotle Translated into English — Politics Book VIII* (Translated by Benjamin Jowett) Clarendon Press, Oxford 1952

ARNOLD, Matthew. *Selected Prose.* Penguin Books 1970. My ideas on advertising, broadcasting, and education in general have been profoundly influenced by him

Arthur Mee's Children's Encyclopaedia. Educational Book Company, London 1930

BARBER, C.L. *The Story of Language.* Pan Books, London 1977

*BARNETT, Lincoln. *History of the English Language.* Sphere Books, London 1970. An American's view. Packed with facts lucidly presented

BARZUN, J. *Simple & Direct.* Harper & Row, New York 1985

BENNETT, Arnold. *Literary Taste.* Penguin (Pelican) Books 1939. Excellent advice from a celebrated Edwardian novelist. Gives detailed instructions for collecting a library of English literature

Bible (The King James). British and Foreign Bible Society, London

Brewer's Dictionary of Phrase & Fable. Cassell, London 1978. A standard work of reference throughout the English-speaking world

British Orations. J.M. Dent, London 1969

BURKE, Edmund. *On taste – On the Sublime and Beautiful – Reflections on the French Revolution – A letter to a Noble Lord.* P.F. Collier & Sons, New York 1969

BRYSON, B. *Dictionary of Troublesome Words.* Penguin 1984

Cambridge Guide To English Literature. Cambridge University Press 1983

CAREY, G.V. *Mind The Stop.* Cambridge University Press 1939

Chambers 20th Century Dictionary. W & R Chambers, Edinburgh 1983. The most comprehensive single-volume dictionary

CONFUCIUS. *The Analects.* Oxford University Press 1955

*CURME, George, O. *English Grammar.* Harper & Row, New York

CUTTEN, Theo, E.G. *"Why Can't the English?"* Hugh Keartland Publishers, Johannesburg 1971. Witty and informative on South African English

DAHL, Roald. *Matilda.* Puffin Books, 1989

DONNE, John. *Complete Verse and Selected Prose.* Nonesuch Press, London 1942

Dorland's Illustrated Medical Dictionary (Twenty-fifth Edition). W.B. Saunders, Philadelphia 1974. For medicos and medical students. An example of impeccable English from America

EINSTEIN, Albert. *Out of My Later Years.* Citadel Publishing, New Jersey 1974

English Language and Literature. Odhams Press, London 1944

EVANS, Harold. *Newsman's English.* Heinemann, London 1972. Advice on journalism by an eminent British editor

FARQUHARSON, Janice. *(1) History as she is wrote in the Transvaal; (2) History as she is tesTED to destruction in the Transvaal; (3) Whose past? How the TED learns you our history.* Business Day, Johannesburg. Articles 13 August, 22 October, 21 December 1987 respectively. An exposé both frightening and hilarious of present-day South African schooling

FLESCH, Rudolf. *How to Write, Speak and Think more effectively.* New American Library 1960

FORD, Henry. *My Philosophy of Industry.* George G. Harrap, London 1929

*FOWLER, H.W. & FOWLER, F.G. *The King's English.* Oxford University Press 1973. A classic

*FOWLER, H.W. *A Dictionary of Modern English Usage.* Oxford University Press 1937 A classic. A standard work

FOWLER, H.W. *A Dictionary of Modern English Usage.* Oxford University Press 1983. Revised by Sir Ernest Gowers

GOLDING, S.R. *Common Errors in English Language.* Macmillan, London 1967

GORDON, K. *The Transitive Vampire.* Severn House Publishers, London, 1985. Memorable for its humour and illustrations

*GOWERS, Sir Ernest. *The Complete Plain Words.* Her Majesty's Stationery Office, London 1977

HENDERSON, B.L.K. *The English Way.* MacDonald & Evans, London 1960

HERBERT, Alan. *What a Word!*

How To Avoid Incorrect English. Hugo's Language Institute, London. First published in Edwardian times

HOWARD, Philip. *New Words for Old.* (1977) Hamish Hamilton

HOWARD, Philip. *Weasel Words.* (1978) Hamish Hamilton

HUDSON, Kenneth. *The Dictionary of Diseased English.* (1977)

HUDSON, Kenneth. *The Jargon of the Professions.* (1978) Macmillan, London

HUGHES, Geoffrey. *Words In Time* (1988) Basil Blackwell, Oxford. A Social History of the English vocabulary

*JESPERSEN, Otto. *Growth and Structure of the English Language.* Basil Blackwell, Oxford 1967. Explains the chief peculiarities of the English language with interesting comparisons with other languages

*JESPERSEN, Otto. *Essentials of English Grammar.* George Allen & Unwin, London 1959. A compendium of a much larger work of his

JONSON, Ben. *Timber or Discoveries.* J.M. Dent & Sons, London 1951. Observations on men and manners

JONSON, Ben. *Volpone.* J.M. Dent & Sons, London 1956

King Arthur And His Knights of the Round Table. Retold by R.L. Green. Penguin (Puffin) Books 1953. For children. Good introduction to *Le Morte D'Arthur*

Longmans English Larousse. Longmans, London 1968. Combines the essential features of dictionary & encyclopaedia. British & American scholarship under French control. A superb combination

*MALORY, Sir Thomas. *Le Morte D'Arthur* (2 Volumes) Penguin Books 1983. First published 1485. A vast and varied work. Not necessary to read from cover to cover, but dipped into will give a fascinating sight of a past English. The writing (and spelling) of this edition is late Middle English. An easy introduction to Middle English. Good preparation for the reading of Chaucer.

MARENBON, John. *English our English.* Centre for Policy Studies, London 1987

McKASKILL, S.G. *A Dictionary of Good English.* Macmillan 1977

McLEISH, K. *Good Reading Guide.* Bloomsbury Publishing, London 1988

MILL, John Stuart. *Utilitarianism – Liberty – Representative Government.* J.M. Dent, London 1962 (Everyman's Library)

MILTON, John. *The Poetical Works of John Milton* (3 Volumes) Bell and Daldy, London 1832

NESFIELD, J.C. *Outline of English Grammar.* Macmillan, London 1972

NESFIELD, J.C. *Junior Course of English Composition.* Macmillan 1964

NESFIELD, J.C. *Senior Course of English Composition.* Macmillan 1963

NESFIELD, J.C. *Errors In English Composition.* Macmillan 1967

*NESFIELD, J.C. *Manual of English Grammar and Composition.* Macmillan 1946

*ONIONS, C.T. *Modern English Syntax.* Routledge and Kegan Paul, London 1971. This is a new edition, edited by B.D.H. Miller, of the renowned *An Advanced English Syntax* of 1903

Oxford Book of English Verse. Clarendon Press, Oxford 1907. Edited by Sir Arthur Quiller-Couch

Oxford book of English prose. Clarendon Press, Oxford 1925. Chosen & edited by Sir Arthur Quiller-Couch

Oxford Classical Dictionary. Clarendon Press, Oxford 1950. Articles on Greek and Roman biography and literature

Oxford English Dictionary. Clarendon Press, Oxford 1989. The supreme dictionary. Twenty volumes plus three volumes of additions. A compact reproduction was made micrographically in two volumes, but it cannot be read without a magnifier.

Oxford Shorter English Dictionary. Clarendon Press, Oxford. Large. Comparable to Webster's New Twentieth Century Dictionary. It is an abridgement of the great Oxford English Dictionary.

Oxford Illustrated Dictionary. Clarendon Press, Oxford 1970. Clear illustrations of the works of man and nature; also entries on famous battles, statesmen, writers, places and much scientific information.

*Oxford Guide To English Usage. (The Little) Clarendon Press, Oxford. Simple and direct on pronunciation, spelling, grammar and usage. Can be carried in pocket or handbag.

*PARTRIDGE, Eric. *Usage and Abusage.* Penguin Books. A mine of quick advice and information. Use as a supplement to Fowler's *Modern English Usage.*

PLATO. *The Republic III.* (Translated by Benjamin Jowett)

PLUTARCH. *Lives* (Translated by Dryden)

POTTER, Simeon. *Language in the Modern World.* Penguin Books, 1966

POTTER, Simeon. *Our Language.* Penguin Books 1964

*QUILLER-COUCH, Sir Arthur. *Cambridge Lectures,* J.M. Dent & Sons, London 1944

RIDOUT, R. & WITTING, C. *The Facts of English.* Pan Books, London 1976

The Right Word at the Right Time. The Reader's Digest, London 1985

ROBINSON, Ian. *The Survival of English.* Cambridge University Press 1973. Shows the glory of English in the past and the shabbiness of it now in religion, politics, business, education. A frightening and shaming account.

RODALE, J.I. *The Synonym Finder.* Rodale Press, England 1981. Comprehensive and easy to use

Roget's Thesaurus of English Words and Phrases. Many editions since its first publication in 1852. A good abridgement by Penguin Books, 1974. Words and phrases grouped according to theme and meaning.

ROOM, A. *Room's Dictionary of Distinguishables.* Routledge & Kegan Paul, London 1981

SMITH, Adam. *Wealth of Nations.* London, 1776.

STEVENSON, Robert Louis. *Memories and Portraits.* Chatto & Windus, London 1912

136

*STRUNK, W. & WHITE, E.B. *The Elements of Style*. Macmillan Publishing, New York, 1972

The New Arthur Mee's Children's Encyclopaedia Waverley, London, 1974

The Penguin Book of English Verse. Penguin Books, 1970

Treasury of Choice Quotations. Virtue & Co., London 1869

*TREBLE, H.A. & VALLINS, G.H. *An ABC of English Usage*. Oxford University Press 1946

VALLINS, G.H. *Good English*. Pan Books, London 1960

VALLINS, G.H. *Better English*. Pan Books, London 1959

VALLINS, G.H. *The Best English*. Pan Books. London 1963

WALDHORN, A. & ZEIGER, A. *English Made Simple*. Heinemann, London 1982

WATERHOUSE, K *On Newspaper Style*. Viking Penguin, London 1982

Webster's New Twentieth Century Dictionary. Simon and Schuster, New York 1979. Large – comparable to the Shorter Oxford English Dictionary. Good illustrations, some in colour. Would be better for being more prescriptive

Webster's New World Lictionary of the American Language. World Publishing 1971. Good in spite of its silly title

World Book Dictionary. World Book, Inc., Chicago 1989. Would be more serviceable to the youngsters for whom it is designed if it were more boldly prescriptive

WRENN, C.L. *The English Language*. Methuen, London 1956. A select bibliography at end of book will be useful to those studying English further

Young People's Science Encyclopedia. Children's Press, Chicago, 1978 Science clearly explained, generally in good English

ZANDVOORT, R.W. *A Handbook of English Grammar*. Longmans, London 1969. For advanced students

Not Recommended

Longman Dictionary of Contemporary English. Longman, London 1978.
Not recommended because needlessly complicated, and shot through with incomplete definitions.

See it on "jettison" – no indication of the main meaning which is *casting cargo and gear overboard to lighten ship or aircraft in time of danger*

QUIRK, GREENBAUM, LEECH & SVARTVIK. *A Grammar of Contemporary English* Longmans, 1972

Probably the biggest book ever on English grammar. Its volume of data is prodigious. It may give joy to earnest gatherers of minutiae grist and heavy technical terms, but I think it totally unsuitable for the type of students I have in mind. But your cast of mind may be the opposite of mine, and you may find it fascinating. Look at it in a library

Glossary

Index

NOTE: Titles are in *italics*.

Words and phrases discussed in the text are in **bold**.

146

147

149